Marketing Your Retail Store in the Internet Age

Bob and Susan Negen

BICENTENNIAL
1807
WILEY
2007
BICENTENNIAL

John Wiley & Sons, Inc.

Published by John Wiley & Sons, Inc., Hoboken, New Jersey.
Published simultaneously in Canada.

For general information on our other products and services or for technical support, please contact our Customer Care Department within the United States at (800) 762-2974, outside the United States at (317) 572-3993 or fax (317) 572-4002.

Designations used by companies to distinguish their products are often claimed by trademarks. In all instances where the author or publisher is aware of a claim, the product names appear in Initial Capital letters. Readers, however, should contact the appropriate companies for more complete information regarding trademarks and registration.

Wiley also publishes its books in a variety of electronic formats. Some content that appears in print may not be available in electronic books. For more information about Wiley products, visit our web site at www.wiley.com.

Library of Congress Cataloging-in-Publication Data:

Negen, Bob, 1956–
    Marketing your retail store in the internet age / Bob and Susan Negen.
      p.   cm.
    ISBN-13: 978-0-470-04393-6 (cloth)
    ISBN-10: 0-470-04393-8 (cloth)
    1. Stores, Retail.   2. Retail trade.   3. Consumers.   4. Internet marketing.
I. Negen, Susan, 1964–   II. Title.
    HF5429.N413 2007
    658.8'7—dc22

2006015973

Printed in the United States of America.

10 9 8 7 6 5 4 3 2 1

With Love to

PEGGY LEACH
without whom this book and our business
would not have been possible.

GORDON AND BONNIE NEGEN
for their unfailing support, including the many "How'd you do today?"
phone calls in the early days of the Mackinaw Kite Co.

CONTENTS

ACKNOWLEDGMENTS

Special thanks to Rich Leach, Matt Mariani, Steve Negen, Randy Gage, all the wonderful participants in the Marketing Mentor Program who let us share in the success of their stores, and most especially our children, Joe and Sam, who have been so patient and understanding while we worked on this book.

INTRODUCTION

F our years ago, the phone in our office rang and on the other end of the line was a guy we'll call Ken. Bob had met him just the day before at one of Bob's marketing programs. Ken was drowning in debt and desperate for help.

Ken had opened his store only two years earlier: a huge beautiful space, filled with top quality merchandise and a talented, knowledgeable staff. During his first year in business he suffered from what I call the Field of Dreams Delusion, "If you build it, they will come." Well, he built it, and he waited, but the customers didn't come.

So the second year he bought advertising like a drunken sailor and before you know it, he had spent more than $40,000. Unfortunately, most of what he bought didn't work. Sure, all that money had generated some sales, but not nearly enough to cover all his costs.

Ouch!

I could hear his pain over the phone line. And I could feel it in the pit of my stomach. You see, I've made all these same mistakes. I've even had the Field of Dreams Delusion! And I've felt the panic of having too many bills to pay and not enough sales to cover them.

That's why for more than two decades I have been a serious student of marketing. Because marketing is the engine that

1

drives massive levels of sales, builds a huge customer base, and gives you the power to immediately put greenbacks in your bank account.

A great marketing plan gives you peace of mind, which was what Ken wanted, and what I knew I could give him. A few days later, I sat down with Ken and in the next hour and a half showed him a whole new way of building his business, a whole new way to spend his money, and a whole new way to look at marketing.

Within three weeks he had launched a promotion that generated $21,788 the first week, $46,923 the next month, and $31,265 the month after that. This promotion ran three months, generated $101,259 in sales, and cost less than $5,000.

Now you know the old disclaimer, "These results aren't typical." But they are possible—if you know what to do. Which is why we wrote this book.

The world is changing dramatically, and many small retailers are finding it difficult to keep up with the change. Business failures for small retail businesses are among the highest of all categories.

Who Should Read This Book

If you own or manage a retail store or plan on opening one some day, this book is for you! It is a book written for retailers by retailers. This is not a generic marketing book. It was written just for you, to help you become a better marketer, build your store's sales, and drop more money to your bottom line.

Just about all of the marketing concepts and tactics in this book can be used in service businesses, too. We have clients in the restaurant business, in the hotel business, in franchise services, and in professional practices. All have benefited from the customer focused marketing philosophy we teach.

But this book was written for retailers, out of a deep love for retail and for all the people who get out on the sales floor and make it happen every day.

Who Are Bob and Susan Negen and Why Should You Listen to Them?

We love retail. Both of us have spent most of our adult lives in retail. Together, we deliver a knockout one-two punch of street smart merchant and sophisticated retail executive.

Susan has worked as executive for retailing giants like Macy's, Bloomingdale's, and Lord & Taylor, has been on the leadership team of a small retail business, and now sees business through the eyes of an entrepreneur and business owner.

In her nearly two decades of business experience, Susan has effectively managed groups of more than 120 employees, has used her expert analytical skills to purchase inventory for both large and small stores, and has worked with hundreds of retail store owners as the leader of her Inventory Mastery Program.

Bob founded the Mackinaw Kite Co., one of the world's first kite shops, in 1981 when he was only 23 years old. He had just graduated from college, loved flying kites, and didn't want to get a "real job."

He spent the next 20 years learning the secrets of successful merchants. He made more mistakes than you can shake a stick at but managed to survive and has earned the status of "battle-tested retail veteran." Among many noteworthy accomplishments, Bob helped create a yo-yo craze that generated more than two million dollars in yo-yo sales. That's a lot of yo-yos!

In 1999 Bob sold the Mackinaw Kite Co. to his brother and business partner, Steve. Together he and Susan started WhizBang! Training to help retailers learn the critical business skills they need to be successful.

Since starting WhizBang! Training, Bob has spoken to tens of thousands of retailers at conventions, trade shows, and dealer meetings. His Marketing Mentor Program has been hailed as "innovative," "exciting," "powerful," and "outside the box that's outside the box" by its participants.

We believe that independent merchants are the lifeblood of most small towns. Their stores are the glue that keeps downtowns together and the downtowns are the glue that holds communities together. But the landscape is changing fast, threatening the very existence of today's independent retailer.

The Bad News

Let's get the bad news out of the way right up front so we can spend the rest of our time together exploring the good news.

The bad news is that nobody needs your store. The fact of the matter is that today your customers can buy whatever you sell over the Internet, 24 hours a day, 365 days a year. Or by calling the 800 number from their favorite catalog and talking to a supertrained customer support person, all while sitting at home in their jammies. Or by shopping around the clock at any one of a dozen big-box superstores within five miles of their home.

It wasn't always like this. For many of you, it wasn't like this when you opened your business. As recently as 30 years ago independent retailers faced very, very little competition.

Thirty years ago the local merchants got almost all the dollars spent on consumer goods by the residents of a town. There were no other options. If there were three hardware stores in town, they split up the hardware dollars. If there were five florists, they split up the dollars spent on flowers. Of course they were in competition with each other, and the best merchants got the biggest share of the dollars, but it's nothing like the competition you face today.

Thirty years ago Wal-Mart had stores in only nine states and had barely caused a blip on anyone's radar screen. Today Wal-Mart has more than 3,700 stores in all 50 states—not to mention numerous other countries around the globe—and has sales in excess of $100 billion a year.

Thirty years ago no one had to get a bigger, sturdier mailbox to hold the 27 catalogs that arrive in the mail every day.

Thirty years ago *no one* had a computer—not at home and not at work.

The personal computer did not exist. It was 30 years ago that Steve Jobs and Steve Wozniak created Apple I, which was nothing more than a bare circuit board.

There was no Internet, no email, no World Wide Web. Customers didn't have the ability to instantly compare prices, services, and products, let alone the ability to carry around a high-speed wireless connection to the entire world in their pocket or purse!

Today there's no doubt that your online competition is *fierce*. Here is a partial list:

- Competitors on websites selling the same merchandise you sell at a deep, deep discount—maybe even below your cost.
- Your suppliers may also sell online. Many manufacturers and wholesalers now have an online retail presence.
- Established, incredibly sophisticated Internet merchants such as Amazon.com and Overstock.com can offer prices and selections you cannot possibly match.
- eBay offers your customers a chance to buy and sell merchandise directly to each other in what is essentially a global garage sale.

And that's just a partial list! It's enough to give you a massive headache.

The Good News

Yes, there is good news. In fact, we believe that there has never been a better, more exciting, or more rewarding time to be an independent retailer. The good news is that even though your customers don't need you, *they want you.* They want to shop with someone they know.

Your single most important, and possibly your *only* competitive advantage is your ability to develop close, lasting personal relationships with your customers. Your customers and your prospects crave a human connection. If you can deliver a great in-store experience and create that personal connection, the big boys and dot-coms won't stand a chance.

Of course, they're trying to build personal relationships, too, but in this area they are at as much of a disadvantage as you are in the low-price wars. They just can't win.

There's no person at Target or Amazon.com or Home Depot who can have the same kind of personal relationship with their customers as you can have with yours. The owner of PetSmart doesn't serve on the same PTA board as their customers, isn't a member of the local chamber of commerce, can't speak to the Junior Achievement group at the high school, and doesn't volunteer at the neighborhood food pantry. The head honchos at Costco can't be out on the selling floor leading their staff and helping their customers.

You *can.*

You probably can't hire expensive store designers, you probably can't afford to manufacture your own merchandise overseas, and you probably can't afford to buy massive amounts of national advertising. But you *can* pour your heart and soul into your business. You *can* do all the little things that make your customers feel truly special. You *can* have a passion for excellence that no manager of a big-box store will ever be able to match.

You *can* compete against the big boys and win!

The New Millennium Merchant

Although the computer revolution that started 30 years ago is still not mature, the novelty has worn off. The information age is fully upon us. The Internet is a part of everyday life for nearly everyone, from tiny children to gray-haired grannies. The dust from the upheaval of the past 30 years is settling, and everyone can see the competitive landscape more clearly.

And there is a new breed of independent retail store owners who see the opportunities that exist in this new world. We call these folks, and we hope you're one of them, *New Millennium Merchants*.

These retailers are determined to keep what was best about yesterday's mom-and-pop stores but aren't afraid to take it up a notch. They are not intimidated by Wal-Mart, the other big-box-category killers, or competition on the Internet. They understand that there are plenty of customers to go around, and they have a plan to get their share.

They have an enthusiasm and optimism that can't be contained. People are attracted to these folks. They want to be around them, they want to come into their stores, and they want to buy from them.

The New Millennium Merchant comes in all shapes, sizes, colors, geographical areas, and industries, but all share certain basic characteristics.

The Marketer's Mindset

If you are a New Millennium Merchant, you understand that there is plenty of money in the economy to support the kind of business you dream about. The market is there. It's a no-brainer. Millions of dollars are spent on what you sell every day—no matter what you sell. They just aren't being spent with you (yet).

You know that the products you sell have value, and your staff gives good service. If you don't believe that your store is the best for your customers, you may want to rethink your career choice. You need to be passionate about giving your customers what they want and need.

When you put these statements together—people want what you sell, and you do a good job of selling it—it all becomes clear. *The only thing standing between you and the supersuccessful business of your dreams is your ability to connect what you sell with the people who want and need it.* In other words, you need to be a marketer.

The New Millennium Merchant has a "Marketer's Mindset." Notice I didn't say "marketing" mindset, I said "marketer's" mindset. The difference is important. One describes what you do; the other describes the kind of person you are.

Having a marketing mindset, attending a seminar or two, and reading an occasional article will help you grow your business, but it will rarely be enough to stimulate the growth you will need to fulfill your wildest dreams. Marketing is the engine that drives sales, and lackluster marketing efforts will result in lackluster sales.

But thinking about marketing as fun and exciting, keeping your eyes peeled for the next cool idea, trying lots of new, innovative marketing techniques, and considering every part of your business from a marketing point of view—that is the *Marketer's Mindset*. And that's what will build your business.

Having the Marketer's Mindset means being aware of what other people in other industries are doing. If your local pizza joint or beauty salon uses a marketing technique that catches your attention, ask yourself, "How can I adapt that idea to my business?" There are very few truly original ideas, but there are many, many great adaptations.

I don't know if it was banks or fast-food restaurants that first came up with the idea for drive-through service, but clearly one influenced the other. And the flash of inspiration to adapt the idea for a completely different industry was just as brilliant as the creation of the original concept.

If all you do is the same thing that everyone else in your industry or in your town is doing, you'll never get ahead. You need to zig when everyone else is zagging. With the Marketer's Mindset you think outside the box, engage your brain, and most of all have fun!

Be a Learner

The New Millennium Merchant is a constant learner. Life is changing at a breakneck pace, and there's no sign of its slowing down. You have to keep up or get left in the dust. And there's no time to re-invent the wheel. Thousands of business owners before you have made the mistakes, figured out what works, and are willing to share their hard-won knowledge with you. Take advantage of it. Work smart, not hard.

There are lots of ways to be a learner. Reading this book is a great one. You can listen to CDs while driving in your car. Your local library has books available for loan. Any bookstore will have more business titles than you can imagine. Read business magazines and newspapers. Subscribe to online e-zines. Sign up for our free WhizBang! Tip of the Week at www.whizbangtraining.com.

There are many business experts who sell learning resources that come with unconditional, money-back guarantees. Spend the money, and if the resource does not provide the value, if the ideas don't pay for themselves almost immediately, return what you've bought and get your money back. You have nothing to risk and everything to gain.

Don't be intimidated by the vast variety of choices. Ask other businesspeople whom you admire what learning resources they use, and start learning.

To help get you started we've put together a Retailer Resources page on our website with links to some of our favorite books, e-books, and CDs for retailers. You'll find information on everything from getting great publicity to easy postcard mailing. As you read the book, you'll learn more about each of the different resources we've found for you. Look for them in the Hot Tip! boxes scattered throughout the book.

Technology Enthusiast

One of the truly defining characteristics of the New Millennium Merchant is the enthusiasm and speed with which you embrace technology. While you are usually early adopters of new technologies, you don't use technology just for its own sake. You understand how to use technology to truly improve your business and strengthen your main competitive advantage—your relationships with your customers. You know how to stay high touch in a high-tech world.

The New Millennium Merchant has a great website that is an effective marketing tool. It's current, interesting, and relevant to your customers' needs. It is *not* ugly, boring, outdated, or unprofessional.

The New Millennium Merchant uses email to stay in touch with customers. Emailing your customers has so many wonderful advantages that we've devoted a huge section of this book to the subject. It's fast, cheap, easy, immediate, and personal.

The New Millennium Merchant has a robust Point Of Sale (POS) system and uses it to its fullest extent. This piece of technology is supercritical because it cuts across almost all areas of your business—sales, customer service, marketing, staff management, inventory control, accounting, assortment planning, and the list goes on.

For the New Millennium Merchant using technology is an exciting, interesting, and important part of building a successful business. Even if you don't know a bit from a byte or what HTML is, you know how to hire someone who does. You understand how to use technology to your advantage.

Hot Tip!

Because having great POS technology is so important we've listed an absolutely topnotch e-book on the Retailer Resources page of our website www.whizbangtraining.com.

This guide to choosing the right POS software is written by a long-time colleague of ours. Many of our clients have used it and loved it. It's filled with amazing information, comparison charts, retailer reviews, and a database of systems by industry. If you're in the market for new POS software—or better POS software—you should *definitely* check it out.

The Other Retailers

So what will happen to the other retailers? The ones who don't embrace technology, become lifelong learners, or develop the marketer's mindset? Not to put too fine a point on it, they will simply go away.

These are the folks who sit around and whine because the economy is bad, or Wal-Mart moved next door, or the bridge into town is under repair. They're the ones who won't change their store hours to make shopping convenient for their customers. They complain that there's not enough time to learn how to use their computer or put in a POS system.

These folks are largely engaged in what we call "hope marketing." They hope that the Fed will slash interest rates to spark spending, they hope that their chamber of commerce will bring more people into town, they hope that their customers will shop with them again. Some of them hope that the weather is good so people head outside; some of them hope that the weather is bad so people head for the malls. Hope springs eternal, but hope is not a good marketing strategy.

Are you going to be a vibrant, successful New Millennium Merchant—or are you simply going to go away? The choice is yours.

We think we know what your choice is. You've picked up this book and are reading it. You're not sitting around blaming slow sales on someone else; you are a learner, you're embracing technology, and you're developing your marketer's mindset!

The WhizBang! Marketing System: Four Steps to Higher Sales and Happier Customers

Most marketing by independent retailers today lacks focus. It's usually a scattershot approach—a little bit now and a little bit then—mostly driven by advertising salespeople. Newspaper, radio, cable TV, yellow pages. When they come and make their sales pitch, the store owner buys an ad. When they don't, not much marketing happens.

If this sounds like you, you're probably spending lots of money on advertising but not getting much in return back at the cash register. You're starting to think of advertising and marketing as an expense, but it's not. It's an investment.

Great marketing is an investment in building your business that pays you back big time. Without great marketing you don't have the engine that drives sales and keeps your company thriving and growing year after year after year.

WhizBang! Marketing is a focused, systematic approach with four steps that will lead you to higher sales and happier customers. And it will cost you a lot less than the scattershot approach.

With this system you will think about the life cycle of your customer—kind of like the butterfly life cycle diagram you drew as a kid. Remember the circle with the arrows?

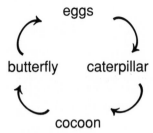

Well, with this system you're going to start at the beginning of your customers' life cycle with your business and try to keep them alive and buying from you over and over for as long as you possibly can.

Different kinds of marketing work best for customers at different stages in their relationship with you and your store, different stages in their customer life cycle. You need to use some of each kind for your marketing efforts to be the most effective and give you the biggest bang for your buck.

There are four steps to the system.

Step One: How to Get New Customers without Going Broke

Every business needs a steady stream of new customers. This is where most people focus the majority of their marketing attention and spend the majority of their marketing dollars. They buy ads because they don't know what else to do or how else to reach out to their prospects. We think there is a better way—a much cheaper way. In this book we give you six low-tech tactics and six high-tech tactics for getting new customers.

Step Two: Turn a First-Time Buyer into a Regular Customer

This is a critical stage in your relationship with your customer. If you could insure that every first-time buyer turned into a long-term customer, what would it mean for your store? We show you how to get the job done with three low-tech tactics and two high-tech tactics.

Step Three: Get Your Customers to Shop More Often

Now the fun begins! This is the stage when you can take full advantage of your number one competitive advantage—building great customer relationships. *Step Three is where the big money is!* We're offering you four low-tech and four high-tech tactics to keep the money flowing into your business.

Step Four: Keep Your Customers for Life

And we do mean life. Wouldn't it be great if all your customers continued to buy from you until they died or moved away? Of course, there are other reasons customers stop shopping with you. The trick is to keep them with you as long as possible. You'll find three terrific tactics to help keep them coming back year after year.

When you approach your marketing systematically you'll be able to create a plan that fits your budget, works for your business, appeals to your customers, and targets all four of the stages in your relationship with your customers, not just buy some ads from the most persuasive salesperson.

In other words, you'll have a plan that works.

How to Use This Book

First and foremost, we hope you'll read this book with pen in hand and highlighter at the ready. Scribble notes in the margins, underline the parts you like, highlight stuff you want to try in your store. Nothing would please us more than to see your copy dog-eared, tattered, and well-worn. The more you get physically involved by writing or underlining, the more the ideas will cement themselves in your brain.

We've organized this book into four major sections, one for each of the Four Steps. In each section you'll find:

- *Key Concepts*—These are some basic marketing philosophies we think will help you better understand the tactics that follow. This is our way of helping you be a learner.
- *Low-Tech Tactics*—These are the what-to-do ideas for each stage in your relationship with your customers that you can do without any New Millennium technology. Everybody can use these ideas starting today.
- *High-Tech Tactics*—These are the what-to-do ideas using the Internet. Each tactic explores how to use e-marketing to create closer, more personal customer relationships.

Second, because we've been in your shoes, we understand that you have limited time and money with which to accomplish your marketing goals. So we've rated each of the tactics on how much time and money it will probably take and how good it is at relationship building. Here's our scoring system:

🕐 = Takes Very Little Time

🕐 🕐 = Takes Some Time and Effort

🕐 🕐 🕐 = Most Time Intensive

$ = Very Inexpensive

$ $ = Requires Some Cash Expenditure

$ $ $ = Most Expensive

☺ = Gives the Least Personal Connection

☺ ☺ = A Pretty Good Relationship Builder

☺ ☺ ☺ = Creates Great Personal Relationships

For each tactic in the book we give you a combination rating that will show you what you can expect from that tactic. Like this:

Newspaper Advertisement   ⏰ $ $ $ ☾

At a glance you can see that a newspaper ad doesn't take much time, but can be pretty pricey and doesn't deliver much in the way of personal connections with your customers—only half a smiley face!

You'll find a Hot Tip! box wherever we have an outside resource we think every retailer should know about. You'll get a short description so you can decide if it's something you want to investigate further.

Hot Tip!

Learn more about great resources for retailers.

When you see the They Did It box, pay close attention. These are true stories about real retailers (names changed to protect the innocent) who were successful using the ideas and techniques in that section. We've tried to include as many of these stories as possible, figuring that nothing is more inspiring than real-life success.

They Did It . . .

Owners of an Indiana ice cream parlor started a Celebrity Scooper program. Each Monday, from the time they opened in the late spring until school let out, teachers, coaches, and principals from local schools came in and helped scoop behind the counter.

Each school got its own Monday, and 10 percent of that day's sales went back to the school. The owners report that they doubled their Monday sales from the year before, and they donated $4,500 back to their community schools. Plus they report that "more important than the sales increase, which was significant, was the amazing goodwill and publicity it generated."

After the school year ended, they continued the programs for other causes with other Celebrity Scoopers including local law enforcement officials, prominent businesspeople, church leaders, and the mayor. This program helped this business grow more than 25 percent last year!

. . . You Can, Too!

In some instances we've created fictional businesses to help explain how certain tactics might work. We've tried to use types of businesses in these examples that are very familiar to most people—florists, bike stores, gift shops, clothing stores, garden centers, shoe stores, ice cream stores, and so on. We tried to pick the kinds of stores that many people would have had experience with, to make it easier to understand how the tactics we describe would work.

That doesn't mean that these ideas aren't good for all the other kinds of retail stores out there—and most service businesses, too. It's just that if you're not an equestrian, you probably haven't visited a tack shop, so it might be harder to follow an example using that industry.

We've also included two special sections—one on advertising in the traditional media and one on copywriting for retailers. These two extra sections will make all the other tactics we explore even more powerful.

Result: Retail Success

Make absolutely no mistake about it: Building the business of your dreams is possible. Your store can reward you with financial security, an outlet for your creative energies, and the deep sense of personal fulfillment that comes from creating a successful business.

But success doesn't happen by accident. It has nothing to do with luck, and while it may have worked 30 years ago, today sitting around hoping your store will fill up with people is an activity for the soon-to-be-out-of-business.

Success comes from being proactive about building your business, from understanding your competitive advantages, kicking them into high gear, and making something happen.

Let's get started!

How to Get New Customers without Going Broke

Five Key Concepts for Getting New Customers

These five basic marketing ideas are important to understand because they are the foundation for all the tactics that follow. In fact, these five concepts will come into play again and again as you go through this book.

Key Concept #1: Be Willing to Pay to Get New Customers

Unless you're counting strictly on word of mouth or your good looks to bring you business, you're going to have to *pay* to generate a steady flow of new customers.

If you buy an ad in the yellow pages, in a coupon pack, or in the local newspaper, you are spending money to acquire new customers.

If you send a postcard to hot prospects, the cost of the card and the postage buys you new customers. If you're paying big bucks for rent at a high-traffic mall, you're spending money to get new walk-by customers.

Even if you're banking on your good looks to get you new customers, you'll probably have to spend on gym membership, tooth whitening, hip hairstyle, and stylish clothes. They're all costs of acquiring new customers using the good looks tactic!

Here's an example of how much it's costing two fictional store owners to buy new customers.

Money Bags Mark
Gets new customers using regional magazine advertisements.

Cost of Magazine Ad
Ad Design—$250
Cost of Ad—$1,250/month
On average Mark gets three new customers
from each magazine ad.

Total Cost to Acquire a New Customer: $500

Savvy Sam
Gets new customers using a referral system.

Cost of Referral System
Post card—$.75 per prospect
25% off first purchase—
Avg. $7.50
Thank-you card for referrer—
$1.00
Free gift for referrer—
$5.00 Blockbuster card

On average Sam gets one new customer for every 15 postcards sent.

Total Cost to Acquire a New Customer: $51.75

So which business owner is doing the better job of buying new customers? Well, at first glance it sure looks like Savvy Sam has the best strategy (which he probably does), but if the lifetime value of Mark's customers is $27,000 then spending $500 to get a new one sounds like a great deal to me.

And if the lifetime value of Sam's customers is only $63, then paying $50 for a new one seems way too steep. Remember the old adage you get what you pay for? Cheapest is not always best. You are sometimes better off spending a little more and getting better customers (those who will spend more and continue to buy from you again and again) than spending less and getting low-quality customers (one-time buyers of your lowest-priced products or services).

The trick, obviously, is to buy the most good quality customers for the least amount of money. Just because you *can* afford to spend $500 to buy a customer doesn't mean it's not better to spend less. And there's no doubt that most of us can't afford to spend that much. That's why the next section of the book is focused on lower-cost, highly targeted ways to acquire new customers.

Check out Figure 1.1. This gives you a visual frame of reference for thinking about your marketing tools.

Everything in the lower left section is low-cost and very personal. For an independent retail store these tactics are most likely to give you the highest ROI (return on investment). The upper right section is most likely to put you in the poorhouse—very expensive and very impersonal.

Take a look at the four Xs and see if you can figure out which one is:

- A billboard.
- A referral.
- A bag stuffer.
- An endorsed mailing (more on this later).

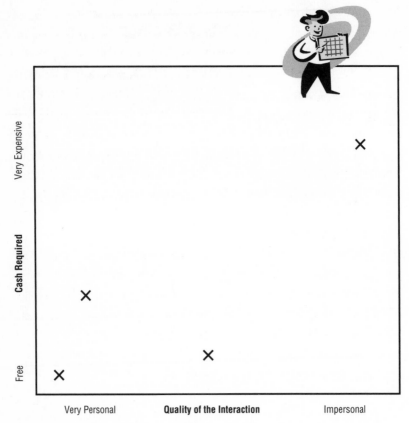

Figure 1.1   Bob's Marketing Matrix.

You might want to take all your marketing tools and plot them on this grid. Do you have too much expensive, impersonal stuff?

Key Concept #2: Understand the Lifetime Value of a Customer

The "lifetime value" of your customer is the total dollar amount they will spend with you before they take their business somewhere else, move away, or die. Customers are not "one-shot wonders."

They are the lifeblood of your business. A good customer will use your services many times over the course of many years and will refer their friends, family, and business associates to you.

Shortsighted businesspeople like to make the fastest possible dollar in-and-out. Smart businesspeople do everything they can to nurture relationships and increase the lifetime value of their customers.

You may not have the sort of detailed records you need to determine the actual average lifetime value of your customers. Most businesspeople don't. But that shouldn't stop you from building long-term, even lifelong relationships with your new customers and perhaps starting to keep track of that information.

Eventually you'll be able to figure out a dollar amount value that an average customer spends on your services over a period of years. Remember: It's the average that's important. Some customers may be worth only $50 to your business over their lifetime, but some may be worth $5,000. It's the average that's important.

Once you know how much each new customer is worth to you, you can decide how much you are willing to spend to get a new customer.

Key Concept #3: Break Even on the Front End, Break the Bank on the Back End

If you put the first two concepts together—you have to pay to acquire new customers and there is a lifetime value to your customers—you come up with this third concept.

Although you still want your overall marketing effort to have an immediate return, acquiring new customers at a breakeven, slight profit, or even a slight loss is now part of your game plan. You'll break the bank on the back end through the lifetime value of that customer.

If you know that your average customer is worth $500 a year

and you'll be able to hang onto them as customers for at least five years, you have an average customer whose lifetime value is worth $2,500 ($500 \times 5 = 2,500$).

It comes down to this: What are you willing to give up to get that person as a new customer? Twenty dollars? Fifty dollars? One hundred dollars?

Because most retailers don't look past the first transaction, they aren't willing to give anything up on the first transaction. They think they are "giving it away" and they *hate* giving it away.

Once you understand that the real value in the customer comes *after* the first transaction, it just makes sense to make some sacrifices to get the first sale. You can shift your thinking from "Get a customer to make a sale" to "Make a sale to get a customer."

Key Concept #4: Apply the "Rule of Reciprocity"

In the following sections that describe some of our favorite tools to get new customers, you will be hearing a lot about *giving* gift certificates, *giving* to charity, and *giving* gifts to your customers, so I am addressing the giving concept right up front.

An incredibly wealthy and wise man, who is also a supersavvy marketer, once shared his life philosophy with me, and I am going to share it with you. "*Givers Get.*"

This is due, in part, to an unwritten social rule called the "rule of reciprocity," which says that we should try to repay what another person has given us; in fact, we feel almost compelled to do so. If we do something good for someone, they want to do something good for us. If we give something to someone, we will get something in return.

This is why when two people walk through two sets of doors and one person holds the first door for the other, that person will in turn hold the second door for the first person. It's also why a grumpy guy doesn't want you to do him a favor because he'll feel like he owes you.

There is probably a larger metaphysical influence at work when you put the law of "givers get" into play, which some may call karma, some may call God, or some may call "The Force." But that's a much bigger subject than we are tackling today. Just know that it works.

When you deeply and truly understand this concept, you will realize that being an honest, caring businessperson who puts the needs, wants, and desires of the customers first is the only true way to succeed in the long term.

As businesspeople, this means that we don't look at our customers like they are a piece of fresh meat with a checkbook. We look at them and think, "If I do my absolute best for this person, they will reward me for it."

Sure there are businesses out there screwing their customers right and left, and they appear to be successful. Treating customers poorly may result in great short-term business performance, but never in long-term success.

Those companies will never, ever generate the type of loyalty that comes from treating your customers right the first time and every time. Such companies will never develop those wonderful long-term relationships that are the foundation of any truly successful business. Embrace this truth and watch your business grow.

Key Concept #5: Leverage the Power of Affinity Marketing

Affinity Marketing is a powerful way to reach prospective customers quickly, easily, and best of all, cheaply. If you have affinity with someone or something, you are like-minded, have shared interests, or are sympathetic to their causes.

If you have a Harley Davidson dealership, your best affinity probably isn't with 80-year-old women. Now don't you all write us about your Great Aunt Lucy who turned 83 last month and still tears it up on her Hawg; most 80-year-old women aren't buying Harleys.

A much stronger affinity would be with affluent 50-year-old men. An even stronger affinity might be with affluent 50-year-old men who own a boat or a snowmobile.

Lots of retailers focus their marketing efforts on everybody—and nobody in particular. This is part of the problem with newspaper advertising. You're just lobbing something out there to the entire world of possible customers and hoping that someone who is interested sees it.

Figure 1.2 shows the world of possible customers. The center dot represents the people who are already your customers, the middle ring represents your hottest prospects, and the furthest ring out is the rest of the world.

If you choose marketing opportunities that are focused on your hottest prospects (people who are predisposed to buy your products

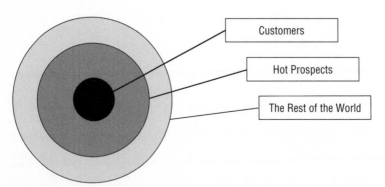

Figure 1.2   **The World of Possible Customers.**

and services) and avoid the ones aimed at the entire world of possible customers, you'll spend less and sell more.

Precision = Profit

The more precisely targeted your marketing is on customers who already have an affinity for your business, the more profitable it will be. It just makes sense. Spend your marketing dollars on the people who are most likely to buy from you. *The trick is to find large groups of those people and invite them into your store.*

The best way to do this is to seek partnerships with other businesses whose customers already have an affinity for your store. You want to find the companies whom you share customers with. Ask yourself these questions: "Who else has the kind of customers that I want to attract to my business? Who else has customers who would be interested in my products and services?"

You will also want to think about both the "demographics" of your best customers—where they live, how much money they make, how old they are—as well as the "psychographics" of your best customers—what their hobbies are, what they believe in, what's important to them.

Here's a sample list we created for a group of national furniture repair and refurbishing franchises. It will give you an example of how many you can and should come up with. The two questions we asked were:

1. Who else provides home beautification services to affluent home owners?
2. Who else provides services to successful businesses with public offices?

Residential Partners	Business/Commercial Partners
Carpet Cleaners	Accountants
Furniture Stores	Lawyers
Financial Planners	Office Supply Stores
Realtors	Computer Dealer/Repair
Garden Center/Florists	Bookkeeping Services
Appliance Stores	Commercial Cleaning Services
Handyman	Office Furniture Stores
Insect/Pest Removal Services	Office Equipment Dealers
Housewares Stores	Art Brokers
Grocers	Travel Agents
Car Dealers	Banks
Dentists	Commercial Realtors
Chiropractors	Caterers

I came up with 26 different kinds of businesses that might have customers who would be great partners for these furniture repair franchises. Didn't even take very long. Here are some more examples:

A *carpet store could partner with* carpet cleaners, furniture stores, realtors, car dealers, interior designers, art galleries, home décor/gift shops, kids' clothing or toy stores, veterinarians, pet stores, paint stores, lighting stores, or appliance stores.

A *hair salon could partner with* women's clothing stores, massage therapists, dentists who specialize in whitening, jewelry stores, shoe stores, cosmetics stores, fitness centers, eyeglasses providers, accessories stores, spas, health food stores, or cosmetic surgeons.

A *florist could partner with* a housewares store, interior decorators, men's clothing stores, gourmet food shops, caterers, party supply/rental stores, jewelers, women's clothing stores, or art and framing galleries, party planners, a garden center, a candy store, a bakery.

An audiologist could partner with optometrists, dentists, chiropractors, massage therapists, beauty salons, cosmetic surgeons, cosmetics stores, pharmacies, or any other medical care provider, the local senior center, churches, mosques, and synagogues, travel agencies.

A toy store could partner with a book store, kids' clothing stores, public libraries, shoe stores, sporting goods stores, kids haircut places, kid-friendly restaurants, skating rinks, bowling alleys, art supply stores, camps, orthodontists, obstetricians, pediatricians.

Make your own list here.

_____   _____

_____   _____

_____   _____

_____   _____

_____   _____

_____   _____

_____   _____

_____   _____

_____   _____

In the next sections on the specific tactics you can use to get new customers without going broke, you'll find lots of ways to use this list. And you'll probably think of many more groups you share customers with. Add them to your list.

Six Low-Tech Tactics to Get New Customers without Going Broke

The next six ideas for getting new customers are practical, proven, profitable techniques we have used with our clients over and over again. These low-tech tactics don't require any fancy technology and aren't dependent on the Internet to work. They focus on starting close customer relationships and laying the groundwork for a solid future together.

New Customer Tactic #1: Give Away Gift Certificates

Giving away gift certificates to use in your store is a simple, fun way to get new customers. I use gift certificates in conjunction with many of my other new customer tools, so here are the basics of giving gift certificates, before getting into the details of the other tools.

A gift certificate is a coupon on steroids.

Gift certificates are significantly more powerful than coupons for two very specific reasons:

1. *The quality of the gesture.* Everyone likes to get something for free. When you give someone a gift certificate, they correctly see it as a generous gesture, a *gift*. It's a sincere invitation to visit your store or business and check out your goods or services. You're putting your best foot forward.

On the other hand, most people see coupons as a thinly veiled sales pitch, so they judge the quality of the coupon solely on the quality of the offer. And the quality of the offer is determined only by the savings involved. It's driven entirely by price. There is absolutely no loyalty building, no relationship building, no "Wow, that's nice of them" involved with coupons.

2. *People treat coupons like trash; they treat gift certificates like cash.*
Now, I know the world is filled with coupon clippers. But there are just as many people who have never clipped a coupon in their lives. Most coupons go directly into the trash can. But even those people who don't clip coupons hold onto gift certificates. They are treated as if they are cash. In fact, most people we know have one, two, or several gift certificates hanging around, just waiting to be used.

Now, you may be cringing, thinking "I *hate* giving stuff away; it kills my margins," or you may feel like you can't afford to give away anything, but let's take a look at it a little closer.

Giving away gift certificates is really a supersmart way to acquire customers at a very reasonable cost with very little risk. It costs you almost nothing to give away the gift certificates, and (here's the part we really love) it doesn't cost you anything if they don't use the certificate. You pay only for the customers you actually acquire! Just try negotiating a deal with your local newspaper where you pay only if your ad gets you new customers.

They Did It ...

A Midwest client with a chain of ice cream and candy stores was opening a new location and, rather than buying advertising in the local media, he sent five-dollar gift certificates to all the homes within a five-mile radius of the new store.

He spent $5,200 on design, printing, and postage. Twenty-seven hundred people came in and redeemed the gift certificates, spending almost $30,000.

"This was one of the most successful promotions I've ever done. Those gift certificates were burning holes in those people's pockets!" he commented enthusiastically.

... You Can, Too!

Three Common Questions about Giving Gift Certificates

Q: *What is the right amount for my gift certificate?*

A: It depends on your average sale. If your average ticket is hundreds of dollars, a five dollar gift certificate is not going to bring a stampede of customers to your store. But if you own an ice cream store, it might. A good rule of thumb is to make your gift certificates between 25% and 50% of your average sale. If you keep the gift certificates less than half of your average sale, and your cost of goods is more than 50%, the worst you'll do is break even.

Keep testing. Give away some certificates at $20 and then some at $10 and compare the results. Compare the redemption rate, the average sale, the buzz that each created, what type of customers they were drawing in, and so on. Don't assume that the bigger denomination is always better. We have two clients who have tested both $5 and $10 certificates and find they get better response with the $5! Got to love that.

Q: *How much fine print should I put on my gift certificates?*

A: As little as possible. Remember, this is a gift and every condition you put on the gift takes away from the value of the gesture.

Absolutely don't do the old "$5 off with any purchase of $20 or more" because you've just changed your wonderful gift certificate into a coupon in disguise—and it won't fool anyone. They'll immediately think, "$5 off on $20: The best I can do is 25% off, so how can I spend as close to $20 as possible to get the biggest discount?" In fact, you're rewarding them for spending the least possible amount rather than for spending more!

You could put a statement on every certificate (in small print) saying, "Please, only one certificate per purchase." This prevents several people from pooling their gift certificates together to make a big purchase using your gift certificates.

Q: *Won't people take advantage of my generosity? Won't somebody screw me?*

A: Of course they will. But don't let that discourage you or distract you from the fact that the goodwill you are generating, the new customers you are bringing into your store, and the cold, hard cash coming from those customers far, far outweigh the problems created by the few knuckleheads who will spend $9.99 with a $10 gift certificate. If too many people are taking advantage of your generous offer, it's time to take a hard look at whom you are giving your gift certificates to. Remember, you want to get your gift certificates into the hands of people you want to be your customers, not a group of knuckleheads.

When evaluating the success of your program, you'll find it's all about the averages. If the average sale from your gift certificate program is paying for the program, you're way ahead. So it is important to track your average sale. An easy way to do this is to have your sales crew write the total amount of the sale (before GC) on the back of each gift certificate. Or you can use a simple tracking form like the one in Figure 1.3. Then at the end of the day/week/month you can add up the number of gift certificates redeemed and check your averages.

If your average sale is at least twice the amount of your gift certificates—the cash you collect pays for cost of the merchandise—then you have broken even on the promotion, which I see as a big success.

In effect, you have succeeded in acquiring a new customer for nothing! The real money comes from keeping that customer and

Date	Customer Name	Total Sale	$ Gift Cert.
4/27	Susan Smith	$127.83	$50.00
4/30	Leslie Banks	$248.00	$25.00
5/1	Pat Jones	$ 75.26	$50.00

Figure 1.3   **Gift Certificate Tracking Form.**

selling them lots of stuff for many, many years. Don't forget: In the long run, givers get.

There are many ways to use gift certificates in your marketing, and we go into many of them in depth in the following sections. But one simple, fun, effective way is just to hand them out to people you meet.

Don't ever go to a networking event, a business luncheon, or a charity fundraiser without a fistful of gift certificates. Aren't you always amazed at how many people will, once they find out you own a particular store, say something like, "Oh, right! That looks like such a cute little place. I've never been in there!" or "Wow, I didn't even know there was a bike store on Third Avenue!" Invite them in and give them a gift certificate so they know you mean it.

Handing out gift certificates is much more fun—and memorable—than giving a business card, and you won't believe how many people will actually come in to redeem it. Bingo! You've got yourself a new customer.

They Did It ...

Owners of a Midwest ice cream parlor give away one-dollar gift certificates to everyone and anyone in their small town. They have contests to see which employees can give away the most. One of the owners is also a school bus driver so every kid in the school system gets one. They give them out with their tip when they eat at a restaurant, and a local church gives them out to the kids who go to Bible School. They enthusiastically distribute them all over town!

The very happy owner reports, "The average sale from the person who brings in the gift certificate is in the $4.00 range and our food costs are 30% so we're still making good money from each sale. Plus, hardly anybody eats ice cream alone, so they bring their friends, who pay full price. It's hands down the best way we've used to grow our business!"

... You Can, Too!

New Customer Tactic #2: Send Endorsed Mailings

One of my absolute favorite ways to partner with the businesses with whom you share customers is to use the endorsed mailing technique. An endorsed mailing gets other businesses to promote your goods and services to their customers.

Instead of contacting your prospects cold, you are given a warm introduction. You're taking advantage of the (hopefully) close, personal relationships your partner business has with their customers. This is one of the best ways we know of to get your gift certificates into the hands of your hottest prospects. It's the perfect synergy of "givers get" and affinity marketing.

Here's how it works. Take a look at the list of affinity businesses you listed earlier. Decide which business you'd most like to partner with and approach the owner or manager. Ask if they would be willing to share their customer list with you.

Explain that you'd like to send a letter to their customers with a message *from them,* (not you) on *their letterhead,* in their business envelope. The letter will include a "thank-you for being my customer—here's a gift for you" message, a gift certificate for your store, plus any other marketing materials you want to include, like your brochure or catalog.

But why would anyone share their customer list with you? Simple.

- They provide their customers; you provide their customers with something of value.
- They get a very powerful marketing piece sent out to their customers for free; you get new customers.

It's a win-win situation!

Here's the trick. You have to make it a no-brainer for people to partner with you. You do all the work; you pay for the stamps, print the letters, and stuff the envelopes. You provide the gift certificates and information about your business. All your partner has to do is give you a database of names (or labels), a stack of letterhead stationery, and envelopes.

We have seen this technique immediately generate tens of thousands of dollars and even much more—not to mention the long-term lifetime value of the new customers you're getting. And the more partner businesses you have working with you, the better. So start by approaching your best potential partners and then spreading out from there.

They Did It . . .

Remember our desperate friend Ken from the very beginning of the book? The guy who spent $40,000 on advertising and hardly got anything, then took Bob's advice and turned a $5,000 investment into more than $100,000 in sales?

He did this by doing an endorsed mailing with several local businesses. Ken partnered with financial planners, builders, and even a shoe store.

Since he owned a garden center, he wanted to make sure lots of people got the gift certificates during the early spring when he had the best opportunity to sell them their spring lawn and garden supplies, so he sent his endorsed mailing in mid-April.

He commented, "Not only did the endorsed mailings start the spring out with a bang, it brought *lots* of new customers in my doors. This costs much less than any of the advertising I did last year and got many times the results. I love it!"

. . . You Can, Too!

New Customer Tactic #3: Partner with a Charitable Cause

You can take the concept of endorsement and make it even more powerful by working with local nonprofit agencies and other worthwhile causes. It's called *Cause Marketing*. The idea is to work with a cause, usually a local nonprofit organization to raise money for the organization, while raising your profile in your community and acquiring new customers.

Here's the gist of it: The charitable organization gives you access to their member list, and you donate a percentage of all the sales their members generate for your business. There are a number of variations on this basic theme.

First, decide which types of organizations would make good partners for your business. Try to connect with organizations that your customers are likely to respond to. For example a garden center might partner with the local Land Conservancy group or an audiologist might work with the local chapter of the Association for the Deaf and Hearing Impaired. Or pick a local charity that everyone could support, like a food pantry. Or pick a cause that you personally feel strongly about or have some connection to, like fighting breast cancer or finding the cure for diabetes.

Whatever you do, try not to pick groups that may alienate big chunks of your customer base. Working with the National Rifle Association (NRA) would be great if you have a gun store but probably not if you own a health food store. Same with political or religious organizations—you may want to use caution.

Think of a list of causes and nonprofit groups that you can work with. Include both local (because people love to give close to home) and larger groups.

Here's the great thing about partnering with a cause: The people who are members of the organization are usually passionate about the cause or the goal of that organization. If they know you are affiliated with their organization, they are likely to become loyal, devoted customers.

Here are several ways to partner with charities and nonprofits that will bring you new customers and give them much needed funds.

Send an Endorsed Mailing with a Charitable Partner

Do an endorsed mailing similar to the one described in the earlier section. Send a mailing to everyone on your partner organization's data base with a gift certificate and a letter telling them that a certain percentage of their sale (minus the amount of the gift certificate) will be donated to the organization. The letter goes out in the organization's envelope, on their letterhead, and the letter is signed by someone in their organization. Again, though, you do all the work and incur all the costs.

An easy way to do the endorsed mailing is to make the gift certificate part of the organization newsletter. If it is sent out in an envelope, the gift certificate could be a separate piece of paper; if it is in a self-contained mailer, it could be part of the body of the newsletter, and the member would have to cut it out before redeeming it.

It's easier for everyone to include the gift certificate with a newsletter, but the response probably won't be as good as if you send it alone because it will have to compete with all the other information in the newsletter.

In this program:

- Your partner endorses you and your store to their membership.
- You give a percentage of the sales generated through the redemption of their special gift certificates.

Throw an After-Hours Gala

A relatively easy way to work with an organization is to invite all the members of the organization to come to an after-hours event at your store. Make it fun; make it glamorous; make it a fashion show; make it a theme party—just make it something people will want to come to.

Donate a portion of all your sales that evening to your partner organization. This is a great one to do right before the holidays; get their holiday dollars for your store before they spend them somewhere else. And do some good in the process.

This is one format in which you might be able to partner with a more controversial organization since all the shoppers at the party would be from the same group. For example, you might have an event for the Republican Party one night and the Democrats another. (After all, you can take money from both.)

The advantage of this type of promotion is that it is very inexpensive, and your support is very visible to the members of the organization. The only real cost involved with an event like this is the extra payroll and some wine and cheese.

With this program:

- You host the party.
- Your partner promotes the party.
- Your partner gets a percentage of the sales made during the party.

Have a Time-Sensitive Partnership Promotion

Lots of organizations have fundraising campaigns, usually ending with an event of some sort, like a banquet, an auction, or a picnic. For example, your local United Way probably has a fundraising push every fall for a couple of months. In this type of promotion you give back a percentage of any of the business that comes from supporters of your partner organization *during the specific time period of the fundraising campaign*. This could be a weekend, a week, a month, or a season depending on how long their fundraiser lasts.

One catch is that the customer has to tell you they are shopping as part of your partnership in order for the organization to be credited with the sale. This lets you know how much your partnership is impacting your sales.

This kind of program is a great way to get your partnership started, and if it does well (they send you lots of business and you donate much money), you'll get lots of recognition during the program at the end of the fundraiser.

With this program:

- Your partner promotes the program and sends its members in to shop with you as part of its fundraising campaign.
- The members who shop with you tell you they are with the organization, to ensure that a percentage of their purchase gets donated to the organization.
- You present the group with a check when the fundraising period ends.

Set Up a Perpetual Partnership Program

In this program you give a percentage of any business that comes from the supporters of that organization back to the organization on an ongoing basis.

This program works well with partners whose members have a strong affinity to your products and you want to wrap up all their business. You don't want them to ever choose any other source over your business. For instance, a garden center could set up a Perpetual Partnership Program with the local garden club. Or a local framing shop or art gallery could set up a program with the local arts council.

Again, the customer has to tell you they are shopping as part of your partnership in order for the organization to be credited with the sale. Creating a Club or issuing a card to the members of your partner organizations makes it more comfortable and easier for your customers to request that the purchase be credited to their group.

For example, The Great Garden Center might create a card like the following one.

The Great Garden Center
Give-Back
Give Back 10% of My Purchase to the
Kalamazoo Garden Club

The card is presented to the salesperson at the time of the sale. There might be details of the program on the back or an explanation of why your business supports their cause. It should absolutely have all of your contact information. A card is also great because it gives the organization something concrete to send to their members when they are explaining and promoting the program.

In this program:

- Your charitable partner promotes the program to its members, possibly sending them your program card.
- You give a percentage of all the sales that come from members of a particular organization back to the organization.

The program remains in place until either you or your partner chooses to discontinue the relationship. Of course, the idea is that both you and your partner organization are making so much money you wouldn't dream of discontinuing it.

The 5% Program

This program is a little bit different and requires a different type of commitment from you. In this program you give a percentage of every sale in a particular department or on a particular service back to any qualifying organization *of your customers' choice*. You let your customer decide where the donation is going!

With this program:

- You set up the partnership criteria, for example: "Our partners have to be 501c3 tax-exempt nonprofit organizations in these three ZIP codes."
- You choose which products or services qualify for the program. For instance, one of our clients offers the 5% Program on custom framing purchases, but not on home accessory or gallery purchases.
- You promote the program to all the potential charitable partners who fit your criteria. Ask them to send their members to you in exchange for a donation.
- Your partners promote the program to their members.
- You promote the program aggressively with in-store signage, in your newsletter and email communications.
- If a customer is affiliated with a charitable organization that isn't yet one of your partners, encourage them to promote the program to their organization as a great way to raise money.

Done correctly this type of promotion is very "viral," meaning it can grow quickly through word of mouth. By the way, 5% is an entirely arbitrary number. If you think 20% would be a more appropriate donation given your customer base, margins, and sales, have at it. Five percent is what we've used with several clients in a couple of different industries, with good results.

Our Favorite Cause Marketing Idea Whose Time Has Come

We love downtowns. We've had stores in downtowns, Bob is involved with the downtown organization in our hometown of Grand Haven, Michigan, and in general we think downtowns are wonderful places to have a retail store.

This is an idea Bob developed while working with several downtown groups. It is kind of a cross between "Throw an After-Hours Gala" and the "5% Program" on a citywide-scale. Here are the basics:

- Your downtown organization throws a big party for all the non-profit organizations in the community as a thank-you for all the good they do.
- The participating downtown merchants agree to donate a percentage of sales generated that night to the charity of their customers' choice.
- The nonprofits invite all their members, supporters, and volunteers to the party.

Make this party fun, fun, fun. Block off Main Street and put up a tent, serve hot cider and donuts, have a strolling brass band, stage a performance of the local high school drum corps, give awards—do anything to make the party festive and inviting. This is a great chance to show off your downtown shopping district. Here are the details of how it works.

Give your event a snazzy name, and schedule it for a *Friday or Saturday night one or two weekends before Thanksgiving*. This is important! Choosing a time several weeks before Thanksgiving has big benefits for all three participants in the event: the merchants, the charities, and the shoppers.

The shoppers are buying (and therefore creating donations for their favorite charity) at a time when they really need to buy—right before the holidays. The organizations are likely to get larger donations because the shoppers are doing their holiday shopping. And you, the retailer, are getting the shoppers into your store early in the season and getting first crack at their gift-giving dollars. Not to mention tons of foot traffic, sales, and new customers.

The downtown group organizing the event sends an invitation to participate to every 501c3 organization in your town and any appropriate outlying areas. Explain that the event is a Thank-You designed to increase their exposure in the community and raise money for their organization. All they have to do is promote the event to their members.

You can get a list of all of these organizations by contacting any business in the Mailing or Mailing Services section of your local yellow pages. Or try www.melissadata.com and click on the Lookups tab. You'll be amazed at how many organizations qualify for your party! In our town of Grand Haven, Michigan (population 28,000) there are approximately 145 organizations that have non-profit, tax deductible status. Every house of worship, club, camp, and center for the performing arts qualifies.

To make tracking the donations to each group easier, we recommend that the downtown group that organizes the whole event—usually a merchants group or chamber of commerce committee—manages the process. Create a tracking sheet with the name of the participating store on top and an alphabetical list of all the participating charities below it. Something like the following one.

Bob's Boutique
Is Happy to Donate 10% of Your Sale
To the Charity of Your Choice

❑ Bernice's House

❑ Butler School for the Arts

❑ Center for Women in Transition

❑ Christ Community Church

❑ Grand Haven Garden Club

❑ Humane Society

❑ Lion's Club

❑ Spring Lake Rotary

❑ St. Cecelia's Music Society

❑ The People Center

Check ✓ your charity, attach your receipt, and turn it in at the Chamber tent on the corner of First and Main Street.

When people shop at a business, they check which charity they want the donation sent to, attach their receipts to their list, and turn it in to the event organizers. The organizers then figure out which stores owe how much to which organizations and communicate the information to the stores and groups. The business owners are responsible for writing the checks to the nonprofits. The downtown group can tell how much money their event created in charity donations and can use that in their marketing materials for the next year.

A big promotion like this can be a lot of work, but it returns a big *Win-Win-Win-Win* for the shoppers, the charities, the downtown, and of course, the merchants.

Other Thoughts on Cause Marketing

One of the questions probably percolating in your mind right now is, "How much? How much should I give? What exactly should be the percentage of sales I donate?"

The answer is it depends. The shorter the time frame of the program, the higher a percent of sales you can give. If you're throwing a one-time, three-hour party, you can probably afford to give a higher total percent of sales than if you're doing a perpetual program. In the shorter time frame event you want to spur immediate buying and also make your donation something sizable enough to keep the charity promoting your store to their members. In a longer-term program you're looking to build loyalty on purchases they would probably have made anyway; you just want to ensure they make them with *you*.

Another key part of cause marketing is to make sure you tell your nonprofit partners exactly what you expect from them. You need to let them know that you want them to *actively* and *frequently* let their members know about the program, not just deposit the donation check every month.

One way to make sure this happens is to make it extremely easy for your partners to promote you. Offer to write and create the letters, emails, newsletter blurbs, or club cards so that all they have to do it use them. Although you'll probably want to start small and grow, the best way to get the maximum number of new customers using this strategy is to partner with *lots* of different causes.

Bonus Benefits

While the main benefit of using a tactic like cause marketing is all the new customers you'll acquire for your business while doing good with the money you've spent to acquire them, there are several bonus benefits.

Solves the Donation Dilemma   If you're like most other retailers, you get people coming weekly, maybe daily, asking for donations for their event, cause, auction, raffle—you know the rest. After a while the relentlessness of the requests can wear you down. It's called donation fatigue.

Having a set program for working with charitable causes takes the stress out of deciding what you should do and for which organizations. Have a flyer at the register explaining the ways that their group can partner with your business, and it's easy! They pick a program, start promoting your store to their members, and you get new, loyal customers.

Tax Deduction   No, we didn't forget that you can take your charitable donations as a tax deduction! In fact it's one of the reasons why cause marketing is so attractive. You can buy your new customers for an already relatively low price (the cost of the donation) made even lower because you can usually take another 30 percent off that expense by taking the tax deduction.

Make sure you go over the program with your accountant and review what kind of donations to what kind of groups are tax deductible.

Publicity   As you'll read in a later section, you must have a good story to generate publicity. A business giving gobs of money to help the homeless, or feed the hungry, or provide children with safe child care is a good story. In other words, cause marketing gives you something to crow about!

You can get publicity from your local media, or you can create it yourself. Send out a press release. Put a page on your website listing and linking to the organizations you support. Send an email to your whole contact list telling that you donated more than $3,000 to local nonprofit groups last month. It's okay to toot your own horn about stuff like this; you deserve it!

They Did It . . .

Owners of an Indiana ice cream parlor started a Celebrity Scooper program. Each Monday, from the time they opened in the late spring until school let out, teachers, coaches, and principals from local schools came in and helped scoop behind the counter.

Each school got their own Monday, and 10% of that day's sales went back to the school. The owners report that they doubled their Monday sales from the year before, and they donated $4,500 back to their community schools. Plus they report that "more important than the sales increase, which was significant, was the amazing goodwill and publicity it generated."

After the school year ended, they continued the programs with other causes and other Celebrity Scoopers including local law enforcement officials, prominent businesspeople, church leaders, and the mayor. This program helped this business grow more than 25% last year!

. . . You Can, Too!

New Customer Tactic #4: Create a Referral System

Customer referrals are probably the cheapest, best way to get new, high-quality customers. In its simplest form, a customer referral takes the form of unsolicited word-of-mouth advertising.

Word-of-mouth advertising is when your customers spontaneously tell their friends and family about your store because they have had a great experience—great service, great merchandise, a need has been meet, they had fun, or they felt exceptionally good about their visit.

Yahoooo! We love it, but the problem with unsolicited word-of-mouth advertising is that you have no control over it. It is a form of "hope marketing." You just sit around and *hope* that people are telling their friends about you.

So while you should work toward creating an amazing experience for each of your customers so that they will give unsolicited word of mouth, it's also a good idea to create a *Referral System.* Please note the word "system." This means that you are systematic about *asking* all your current customers who else they think would enjoy your store, needs your service, or wants your products.

It's the systematic asking that makes a referral system much more effective than unsolicited word of mouth at generating a *steady* flow of new customers into your store.

A great referral system rewards the customer who gives you the referral, the prospect who gets referred, and of course, you. Here's ours in a nutshell.

1. *Ask the customer to give you a referral.* This could be at the actual point of sale, or you could send a request in your postsale thank-you note. You could put a referral form into your customer's bag without actually making the verbal request—not as good as asking, but better than merely hoping for unsolicited word of mouth. You could also periodically send a letter asking for a referral and include your referral form.

2. *Give the customer a referral form* that explains the benefits of the program for both her and the friend she refers. A form is important because you want a name *and address* if at all possible so you can contact the prospect. Lots of times your customer won't have her friend's address with her, but she can take it home, fill it out, and send it back to you. Put a stamp on it so it's supereasy for your customer.

   Sometimes you'll get a customer who isn't comfortable giving out the names and contact information of her friends but would still be happy to recommend you. Fine! Just make sure you have extra brochures, gift certificates, and business cards that she can give her friends. You may even want to have all the materials prepackaged in a nice envelope. This kind of direct referral can be even more effective than when you send out the materials yourself.

3. *When you get a referral, send your customer a thank-you note with a little gift.* It could be a gift certificate to your store, a certificate for a pint of Ben and Jerry's ice cream (yes, they do this and you can get them online), or a free video rental gift card. Not something huge, just a token to say, "Thanks!"

4. *When you get a referral, immediately send the referred person a* packet that includes a letter explaining that their friend gave you their name and that he thought they might like your store or services. Also include a brochure with information about your store and a *gift certificate*. This will motivate them to actually come in and try you out.

5. *Track your referral program by tracking your gift certificates.* You really need to track the program by watching how many of the gift certificates come in and figuring out what your average sale is.

There's one thing that holds most people back from using a referral system. They don't know what to say. Asking for a referral seems very easy but is often very difficult when you are actually face-to-face with your customer. Here are the steps for asking for, and getting, tons of really great referrals. This sample script is just that—a sample. Come up with words that *you* are comfortable saying. Make sure that your request is conversational, not a canned speech. A script is only to help you get organized and figure out exactly what you want to say.

> *Confirm that you have completed everything to the satisfaction of the customer.*
>
> *Sample:* "Thank you so much for your purchase. Is there anything else I can do for you? I'm so glad you're pleased with <whatever they bought>."

Ask for a favor.

Sample: "Can I ask you a favor? If you've had a good experience in the store today, I would really appreciate it if you would share the names of some of your friends who might want to learn about <your products>. You see, my very best source of new customers are my current customers. You folks have already seen <how your product or service solves a need for your customer>."

Describe the person you'd like to know about.

Sample: "Do you know anyone who <describe a need someone has that your product fills> or who <describe another need someone has that your product fills>? That's exactly the kind of person who'd like to hear about <your store>.

Reassure your customer.

Sample: "I don't want you to worry that I'll be bugging your friends. I won't. What I'd like to do is send them a $XX gift certificate and some information about <your company>. Here's the letter I'll be sending." (Show copy.)

Review the form.

Sample: "I know it's tough to come up with ideas on the spot, so I'll give you this form to take home. It explains everything and has space for two names and addresses. If you can think of only one, that's just fine, and if you think of more than two, just scribble them in the margins!"

Direct them on how to return the form.

Sample: "Do you have access to a fax machine? (If yes) Great! Let me write my fax number right here for you. When you think of someone who might be interested in my store, just fill out the form and fax it to me. (If no) No problem. This form is designed to be a self-mailer. (Flip the form over.) I've already put my address there for you, and let me just stick a stamp right here. All you have to do is fold it on the dotted line, staple it, and pop it into the mailbox."

Thank your customer. Never forget this step.

Sample: "You know, I really appreciate your help building my business. Thank you."

Sound too complicated?

Referrals are a really great source of high-quality new customers at a low cost, so do *something* more than hope. Here's the simplest referral program I've ever heard of. Not as proactive as what I just outlined, but better than just hoping for word of mouth!

Hand each of your customers two business cards at the end of every sale and say, "If you liked your experience here at Walt's Widgets, I'd appreciate it if you'd tell your friends about us. Thanks."

They Did It . . .

Here's what the owner of one of the most successful framing galleries in the country says about referrals. "We include a referral card with the follow-up letter we send out after every completed order. The card asks the client to give the card to a friend if they have enjoyed our service. It explains that if their friend comes in to frame, the friend will get $25 off the first order, and they (our current customer) will get a $25 gift certificate in the mail. We are fanatical about quickly sending out that thank-you gift certificate when someone new comes in as a referral.

Last year we did more than $50,000 as a result of people being referred to us."

. . . You Can, Too!

Referrals that you generate yourself are a great way to get a steady stream of new customers, and the next technique is a great way to get other businesses to send you referrals.

New Customer Tactic #5: Engage in "Donut Marketing"

Donut Marketing is fun, easy, and just like it sounds—you give away donuts! Or muffins, or cookies, or veggie snacks, or a local delicacy.

Now, the *key* is to whom you give the donuts. Take the donuts to businesses with whom you share customers—specifically businesses who are very closely aligned with yours but whose goods and services don't overlap with yours. A lawn sprinkler service might take donuts to a garden center. A bike store might take cookies to the outdoor outfitters. A framing gallery might take scones to an interior designer. A children's clothing store might take snacks to the toy store. When you give the donuts, you're putting the Rule of Reciprocity into play. You're giving them something, so they will want to help you out in return.

The great thing about this technique is that it doesn't require a lot of time, effort, or preplanning. It's the kind of thing you can schedule on your BlackBerry or PalmPilot, get a reminder in the morning, and do on your way to work that day. Just stop at your favorite bakery, and then swing by your partner business.

When you deliver the donuts the first time, introduce yourself, your services or products, and leave the prospect some brochures and business cards. Ask if they will refer you to their clients if you do them the favor in return.

Make a point of meeting the people who are in contact with your mutual customers—the actual carpet cleaner, the loan officer, the salesperson—not just the business owner. And don't forget donuts for the front desk and support staff. They are valuable people to have in your corner.

Determine a regular schedule and keep bringing those donuts. After your first visit, you'll want to (briefly) schmooze, shoot the breeze, thank them for any referrals they have sent, update them on anything new in your business, and generally be charming. It is a great way to keep your relationship healthy, and make sure they always have enough of your brochures and business cards.

The more businesses you can get sending clients your way, the better. It's all a numbers game. If you have five other businesses each sending you five new customers a year at $200 a customer, you've added $5,000 to your annual sales. You can buy a lot of donuts with $5,000! Of course, don't forget the lifetime value of those 25 new customers!

I know a vacuum store owner who regularly brings donuts (and a stack of business cards) to a high-end appliance store that does not sell vacuums. The appliance store sends the vacuum store owner all the people who come in looking for vacuums. It amounts to significant amounts of business for him every year.

Interestingly, the vacuum store owner can tell when it's been too long since he delivered the donuts. The number of people coming in from the appliance store slows way down. Once you start a relationship with a business, keep bringing them donuts. It's the regular, happy reminder that your business exists that will keep them sending people your way. Because who doesn't like a mid-morning, fresh-from-the-bakery donut?

New Customer Tactic #6: Generate Publicity

One final way to attract new customers to your store is to generate publicity. Publicity is any kind of objective, nonpaid media coverage about your company or products. It can take many forms—from an article about your business in the local paper or a 15-second spot on the 11:00 News, to a guest appearance on *Oprah*.

You can't buy publicity, but you *can* make it happen. Big companies spend mucho bucks hiring publicity experts to position their companies in the national media spotlight. Manufacturers go to enormous lengths to get their products placed in movies, on TV shows, in books, and on the Web.

With a little bit of know-how, a touch of ingenuity, and some good old-fashioned elbow grease you can probably generate all the publicity you need by yourself. We did.

Every year the Mackinaw Kite Co. got front page stories with full color photographs in every newspaper in West Michigan, interviews on regional TV stations, and days' worth of radio coverage. Why? We had a huge, three-day kite festival every spring at the Grand Haven State Park Beach on the shores of Lake Michigan. People came from all over the country to watch, and competitors came from around the world to participate.

One year we had employees (wearing logo emblazoned T-shirts) on national TV yo-yoing in the Macy's Thanksgiving Day Parade. It was great fun, and the local media picked up the story, too.

Over the years we had more articles, interviews, and video segments than you can believe. How did we get all this great publicity? Easy. We knew . . . *the media's big secret.*

Yes, the media has a big secret, and we're about to share it with you: They need news. Content. Something to say.

Your local TV news has to fill up that half hour every single night whether or not something important is happening. The newspaper has to write enough words to fill the paper every day—plus lots extra on Sunday, and dead air is a definite no-no in radio. In other words, they're all desperate for a good story!

If you have a good story, the media will fall all over themselves to talk to you. And write about you. Or put you on TV. So the trick to generating lots of publicity is pretty simple: Figure out what your great story is, and let the media know about it.

How to Write a Great Press Release

One of the best ways to get your story out to the media is to write a press release. But not just any press release will work. Reporters get tons and tons of press releases every day, and most of them are from publicity pros. So if you want to get noticed, you must know at least a little bit of what the pros know. Here are a few tips.

Write Your Press Release for the Reporter   This is probably the most important thing to know about writing a press release. It has to grab the attention of that reporter who is looking desperately for a good story and make them think three things:

1. Hey, now that's something interesting my readers will really want to read about.
2. Whew, it's not going to be hard to write this story—part of it's already done for me.
3. Yah, my boss is going to *love* this one.

That's what the reporter cares about. Their readers and their job. This may come as a shock to you, but they don't care about you, your store, your products, or your website. If your press release comes across as purely promotional or is filled with fluff it will go directly into the trash. If it looks like it might be interesting to the readers or viewers the reporters are targeting, then you might get a read through.

Get a Good Story Angle   A press release is not an ad for your business. To write a good press release you must have a good story angle. Take the example of the Mackinaw Kite Co. and the kite festival we had every year. A local kite business having a kite festival is not a very interesting story angle, so if we sent something out that started "Mackinaw Kite Co. Sponsors 10th Annual Great Lakes Sport Kite Championship" it probably wouldn't generate much publicity.

However, these headlines would be more likely to grab a reporter's attention:

> "Japanese Team Hopes to Win Big at America's Premiere Kite Event"
>
> "50,000 Expected to Crowd Grand Haven Beaches for Windy Fun"
>
> "World's Largest Kite to Fly Saturday in Grand Haven"

It's the story angle that makes the event newsworthy. The story of the Japanese team or the world's largest kite gives the reporter something to write about. Of course, at the end of the press release there will certainly be something about the Mackinaw Kite Co. with the festival information and business contact information.

Make Your Press Release Sound like a Newspaper Article   Your press release should be written in the third person (eliminate the words *I, you, we, our, us*) and make it sound like it's already a news article.

If you want to say something personally in the press release, you can phrase it like this: "According to business owner Bob Negen, the best kite flyers from across the country and around the world will gather at the Grand Haven State Park this Friday." Or you can make it a quote like this: "The Japanese team is definitely the emotional favorite," says event organizer Bob Negen, "but the Chicago team will be giving them a run for their money this Saturday."

There is a certain clipped style and factual orientation that is a hallmark of newspaper writing. You should emulate that style in your press release. A good way to do this is to read lots of articles from great traditional newspapers like *The New York Times* or *The Washington Post*.

By the way, if you do write a good press release, don't be surprised to find all or part of it actually in the newspaper!

Correct Formatting Makes Your Press Release Professional
There is a well-defined, standard format for a press release, and using this format makes you look like you know what you're doing. Here are 10 key points to remember:

1. Write the words FOR IMMEDIATE RELEASE at the top of your press release.

2. Put your complete contact information below the immediate release statement.

3. Write you headline next. *Bold It and Capitalize the First Letter of Each Word*.

4. Before the first line of the first paragraph write the dateline: city, state—date of press release.

5. Make the first paragraph a powerful summary of the story, and capture the reporter's attention. If it's wimpy, they won't keep reading.

6. The text of the press release tells the rest of the story.

7. If the press release takes more than one page, center the word—*more*—at the bottom so the reporter knows there is another page.

8. At the end of the body text write a short paragraph called the "boilerplate" that tells a little bit about the company that is sending the release. Make sure this is factual and not overly promotional.

9. At the end of the press release center the marks ###. This signals the end of the release.

10. After the 3 #s add a line something like "To get more information or schedule an interview please contact Bob Negen at 616-842-4237 (day), 616-555-4237 (cell), or email Bob at bob@whizbangtraining.com

See Figure 1.4 for a completed sample press release you can use as a guide.

For Immediate Release

Contact:
Joe Smith
Joe's Hobby Shop
Phone: 616-555-4237
Fax: 616-555-2977
Email: Joe@Joeshobbyshop.com

City's Largest Monopoly Tournament to be Held Next Month
Over 100 Participants Expected to Set Record

Grand Rapids, MI—July 1, 2007. Joe's Hobby Shop announced today it will host a Monopoly tournament, inviting players to participate in a 10th anniversary celebration of the store's grand opening. The event, slated for July 26–27, coincides with the anniversary of Joe's first weekend of business 10 years ago.

In this "open" format tournament, Monopoly players of all ages will be paired against other participants at the tournament location. Each player will receive a special commemorative premium token from Monopoly for participating in the celebration event. Thousands of Monopoly tournaments are hosted worldwide each year.

(Continued)

Figure **1.4** **Sample Press Release.**

More than 100 Monopoly players from all over the state are expected to participate in the event. "We hope to set a record for the largest Monopoly tournament ever held in Grand Rapids," commented Joe Smith, President of Joe's Hobby Shop. "One of the things that sets Joe's Hobby apart from other stores is our community of players, and we wanted to give our game players a fun way to participate in the 10th anniversary celebration."

The 10th anniversary celebration event will take place at the Grand Rapids Pavilion. For details on start times and participation, please call Joe's Hobby at 616-555-4327. More information regarding the 10th anniversary tournament event will be available soon on www.joeshobbyshop.com.

The Monopoly game, first released in 1935, is available in 80 countries and 26 languages. Monopoly is a trademark of Hasbro, Inc. (NYSE: HAS), all rights reserved.

Joe's Hobby Shop, Inc., has been a leading retailer of hobby-based entertainment products in the Grand Rapids market since 1995.

To get more information or schedule an interview please contact Joe Smith at 616-555-4237; email joe@joeshobbyshop.com.

Figure 1.4   *(Continued)*

To Whom Should You Send Your Release?   If your main objective in generating publicity is to get customers to come to your store or attend your event, send the press release to your local and/or regional media. There's no point in sending your press release via email to every major news organization in the country if what you want are local customers.

Make a list of every newspaper, TV station, radio station, or magazine you want to send the press release to, and then go online

---

Hot Tip!

If you want more in-depth information on publicity, writing press releases, or public relations, you can find it on the Retailer Resources page of our website.

There's a link to a great set of tools designed by a PR pro and created specifically for small businesses that want to "do it themselves."

---

to find the listing of their news departments. It should be relatively easy to find out who is the editor or reporter in charge of the department that your story best fits.

If your story is about the first local church to install audio technology that directly broadcasts the worship service into the hearing aids of congregants, you might want to send the story to the editor at the health desk or to the lifestyle editor. If your story is about a new tax break people can take advantage of if they use your services, you might send the story to the business or finance editor.

Frequently press releases are sent via fax. Call the main desk to get the fax number of the reporter you are interested in. Or send your press release in the mail or by email. Many times the email addresses and phone numbers of the editor or reporter you're interested in are listed right on the website.

Once you have made contacts at the various media outlets, nurture those relationships. Remember that those reporters are always looking for a good story, and if you give them one every time you call, they will be more than happy to give your business tons of publicity.

Publicity versus Advertising

Getting publicity may seem like the holy grail of marketing be-cause, unlike advertising, it's that word we all love to hear: f-r-e-e! Who doesn't love free? We love free.

There is, however, a very important point to keep in mind when you start thinking about generating free publicity. *With mar-keting and advertising You control the message. With free publicity They control the message.*

You can't control what an independent journalist says about you. They might change their mind about the angle of the story or decide not to run it at all.

Frequently the reporter just plain gets it wrong. I can't tell you how many times we have been misquoted or facts about our business been been misrepresented. Just recently a newspaper covered an event at which Bob was the featured speaker. Imagine our surprise when we read in the next day's paper that Bob had sold the Mackinaw Kite Co. for three million dollars! If only it had been true.

It's not that the reporter is trying to lie about you, or make your story worse (or better) than it really is. Usually it's that they don't understand the facts correctly or that they're just in a hurry to hit their deadline, and they make mistakes.

There's Good Publicity—and Bad Publicity

Here's a quick story to illustrate my point. Imagine a grocery store that's having a circus themed promotion to raise money for the lo-cal children's hospital—a brightly colored circus tent in the park-ing lot, pony rides for the kids, a clown making balloon animals, juggling lessons, and free lemonade for all. TV and newspaper re-porters come to cover the heartwarming story. A great publicity event!

Unless:

- One of the ponies bites a child in front of the TV cameras.
- A reporter discovers that BoBo the Clown is a paroled sex offender.
- The tent collapses injuring seven grocery store workers.
- Any one of a thousand other things goes wrong.

Actually, it's still a great publicity event. From the media's standpoint it's probably even better! But for the grocery store—not so good.

Does this mean you should never seek out publicity? Of course not. It just means that you need to be aware of the differences between publicity and advertising. Sometimes controversial publicity can be quite profitable, even though it may not be strictly positive publicity about your business. One great publicity story is about a friend of ours who owns a small freestanding restaurant. It's a longtime favorite of kids and grown-ups alike, serving hot dogs, chili dogs, hamburgers, soup, and fries.

Several years ago our friend decided to spruce up his place inside and out. Inside he put in new booths, fresh white paint, and cartoon caricatures of happy, dancing hot dogs and hamburgers. The cartoons were such a hit that he decided to get bigger versions of the dancing hot dogs painted all over the outside of the restaurant, too.

The local bureaucrat in charge of sign ordinances must not have been a hot dog lover, however. He decided that the dancing hot dogs were equivalent to signs (the business name has the words "hot dog" in it) and cited the restaurant for a sign violation.

Our friend took it to the courts and every time the newspapers, radios, or TV covered his tussle with the sign guy, his sales shot through the roof! Some of the diners came to support him in his battle against the city; some were just reminded that they were hungry for a hot dog when they heard his business name on the radio. He swears that his sales will never again be as high as they were the year he was embroiled in the sign controversy.

A strong statement about the power of the press. Harness it to work for *your* business.

Six High-Tech Tactics to Get New Customers

Not surprisingly, these high-tech tactics for getting new customers are similar to the low-tech tactics mentioned earlier—they just use the speed and power of the Internet to make them even easier and more efficient. Not to mention cheaper!

New Customer Tactic #7: Have a Great Website

(*Note:* This tactic was really hard to rate because you can spend a little or a lot of money on a website, spend a little time on it or a lot of time on it; it can be a great relationship building tool or an awful one. We decided to go with ratings that reflect what we think are the best ways to do a website.)

Internet technology is here to stay, ladies and gentlemen, and hoping that it will go away is a bad marketing strategy. In fact, every day new advancements are making the Internet faster and easier to use. Here are just two examples among many:

1. *Broadband Technology.* You don't really need to know what "broadband" is: All you need to know is that it's making surfing the Web and buying online much *faster and easier* for almost all users. No more waiting around for pictures to load or orders to process.

Because it's now so quick and easy, more people than ever are going online to check you out. If you don't have a website, or if you have a site that doesn't market your business, well, you're missing out big time.

2. *ZIP Code and City Searches.* I doubt that the yellow pages will be around in 20 years. Here's why: Many popular Internet search engines have added a cool new feature that lets people search for products and services right in their own neighborhoods by typing in what they are looking for and then their ZIP code or their city name.

    The first listing when you do this search says "Local results for XYZ products near your town name." When you click, it gives you a list of local businesses with links to their websites that offer the product or service you're looking for.

    It's a mini, *interactive* yellow pages. Customers can check out the websites before they make a call or visit the store. If the customer finds a bad website or can't find the information they want on the website—no call.

    Try it right now by going to www.google.com and typing in "flowers 49417." The first search result you'll see: "Local results for flowers near Grand Haven Michigan." But only two of the five florists we drive by on our way from home to office are listed there.

    This kind of targeted search technology is making it easy for new customers to search you out on the Web, and you'd better be there when they look.

The Truth about Websites

Regardless of what the techies or web gurus say, as a small business your website probably won't bring you vast hoards of customers from around the world, let you compete with the big boys in your industry, or make you rich. It's just not true.

What your website can and should do, however, is be *a powerful tool to attract your hottest prospects and activate your existing customers*. More and more customers are going to go online to get your telephone number, see if you're open on Sunday, find out if you carry a brand of products they are looking for, see what's new at the store this month, or get directions to your store.

Many of your hottest prospects are comparison shopping online before they decide which store to visit in person. They are checking you out, and if what they find online doesn't match up to your competitor's, you could be out of the running.

For example, let's say I want to buy a new mountain bike. One of the things I do is search online for local bike shops. I browse around on their sites (just as I might if I were actually in their stores) to see what bikes they have to offer, check out how knowledgeable they are, how professional they seem, and what kind of postsale service they provide. Just based on that Web experience alone I make a decision about where I will buy my bike. At the minimum, I rule out any places that look like they can't give me a good buying experience.

This scenario takes place thousands, maybe millions, of times a day in your selling area for a huge variety of goods and services. That's why every single store should have a website with a minimum of three to seven pages about their business and possibly many more.

This type of website is basically an e-brochure. It's the high-tech version of the print brochure you give to promote your business to customers. It's also becoming the high-tech version of your yellow pages ad.

So is it worth the cost of a website just to have an electronic brochure? Absolutely. How much would you pay for a magical print brochure that just showed up whenever your customer was wondering about your store or thinking about buying what you sell?

Plus, we think websites don't have to be expensive to be good.

You'll find out lots more about what makes a good website in the following pages.

What about E-Commerce and Selling Online?

Our feeling is this: Most local people won't visit your site specifically to buy from you online, but if they're already on your site you might as well sell them something!

However, you have to be smart and creative about how you use e-commerce so that it's manageable for you and a good experience for your customers. There are many possibilities. Here's an example.

A local bookstore will never compete with Amazon.com, Barnes and Noble or any of the other huge online booksellers on price, selection, shipping, or website recognition, *but* a creative bookseller could leverage their most valuable advantage—the personal relationships their staff has with the customers.

The bookstore could sell only 50 books at a time online, grouped not by traditional category, but by 10 that each of their 5 employees recommend. Customers know the employees personally and will be interested in buying books recommended by their favorite salesperson. Change titles every month.

You don't have to have all the products in your brick and mortar store in your online store. In fact, you probably shouldn't. You'd go nuts trying to keep that many items updated on your website. Sell just your best-sellers online, or if you are a service business, sell related accessories online. Sell just one brand online, or sell a rotating group of seasonal merchandise online. The point is while they are on your site, you might as well try to sell them something!

Let's take a closer look at what makes an effective website for retailers and what are some of the biggest mistakes store owners commonly make when they build their website.

A Solid Foundation: 14 Points to Consider When You're Building Your Website

1. *Have an Updated, Professional Design.* The Web is a very visual medium and the look of your website gives an instant impression to the visitor. If your site looks unprofessional, it gives that impression about your entire business. Your website should look clean, updated, and professionally designed. It doesn't need to be fancy, or flashy, or ultraunique. In fact it's probably better if it's *not*.

Your website design should be straightforward and created to clearly communicate to your customers. One of the biggest and most common mistakes we see people make when setting up a website is to choose their brother-in-law or their tech-junkie teenaged neighbor to develop their site. I can't state it strongly enough: Being technically proficient and knowing how to program HTML or use FrontPage does not make someone a good web designer. These technical minds usually do not have a strong graphic design sense nor do they understand marketing a small business.

Just because I know how to use a paintbrush doesn't mean I can create a beautiful painting, and just because someone has the technical skills to create a website doesn't mean they know how to make it look good or work for your store. Your website is primarily a marketing tool, and your web developer needs to think like a marketer—not a programmer.

2. *Pick Fonts That Are Easy to Read and Use Them Consistently.* This one goes along with point #1, but it's important enough that it warrants its own mention.

Fancy fonts in bright colors or reverse type (light text on dark/bright background) should be used only in large sizes, probably as headlines—if they are used at all.

The most important thing is that your visitor can actually *read* the text on your website. I know it's boring for some of you, but stick to dark letters on white or light backgrounds for the body of your site, and keep your fonts very simple. Try these:

Arial

Verdana

Tahoma

Times New Roman

Bookman

𝔄 line of text like this will drive your web visitors crazy!

This Times New Roman font is much easier to read and won't make your eyes go berserk.

Be sure to watch the fonts and colors on your navigation buttons. If your visitor can't easily read them the visitor is unlikely to click around and explore your site.

Don't use too many different fonts on your website; pick one for headlines and one for the body text, and keep them consistent throughout your site. It's disconcerting for your visitors to move from one page to another in your site and have the font styles, colors, and sizes change. Makes them feel like they're not on the same site. Get yourself a good web designer and this shouldn't be a problem.

3. *Have a Strong Headline.* Your website home page—and all the other pages—need to have a strong headline just like all your other marketing materials. Your store name is not a headline, and "Welcome!" is not a headline. *Your home page headline should tell quickly and clearly what you do and why the visitor should keep on exploring your site.* The headlines on the other pages at your site should highlight what the visitor will find on that page.

We explore more about how to write great headlines in the special section "Copywriting for Retailers."

4. *Avoid Cutesy Designs or Animations.* While dancing dogs or falling leaves may seem fun at first, they usually end up distracting and detracting from the message you are trying to convey to your visitor. Some are downright annoying.

We once visited a website and wherever you moved the mouse, it left a trail of fireworks behind—and this was *not* a website for a fireworks company. For the first 10 seconds it was kind of fun to see the fireworks, but after that this animation made it extremely hard to use the site.

Now, I'm not saying that it's impossible to use animation well and to great effect. I'm just saying that it's hard. You can rarely make a mistake by leaving it out.

This is especially true of looooooong "Flash" animation introductions to your website. The Internet is designed to go *fast*, and if you make your customers wait even five seconds to get into your site, forget it. They'll click that X button so fast your head will spin!

5. *Use Common Words, Not Industry Speak, and Don't Use Abbreviations.* You know what happens when you *assume* that everybody knows what you mean when you say SDU or RFP or CRM, don't you. If you use terms, abbreviations, or phrases that your visitors don't know, they will feel stupid. And they'll leave your site frustrated.

Be sure to write all your web page copy with a generic customer in mind; write conversational, customer-focused copy that explains clearly what you mean. Read the section on copywriting for more on this topic.

6. *Have Your Contact Information on Every Page.* You may not need to have *all* of your contact information on every page, but at least have some basic information on every page. Your store phone number, your email address, the store address. This makes your site

feel like it is actually attached to a physical place and person rather than an anonymous cyber-creation.

Also, when your potential customer has been browsing around and decides to call you or hop into the car and visit the store, you don't want to make them search around for the information. Make it as easy as possible for your customer to do business with you.

7. *Use Consistent Navigation.* Navigation buttons along the top or the side of your site allow visitors to click and move around within your site. It's important that the navigation buttons are clearly labeled. They should look the same and be in the same spot on virtually every page in your site.

Just as you don't want to go to the grocery store and have them move the milk on you every week, your website visitors want to find those navigation buttons in the same place on every page, every time.

8. *Make the Return to the Home Page Easy and Intuitive.* Make sure there is an easy way for the visitor to get back to your home page from every part of your site. Make it easy to find and not tricky. Your site visitors do not want to guess.

Some sites make the "return to home" clicking the company logo at the top of the page, and that's great if it's not the *only* way to get back to the home page. Someplace there needs to be a navigation button with the word HOME on it.

9. *Create Internal Links to Other Pages Within Your Site.* An internal link is a link to another page within your own site. Adding internal links in your text is a great way to keep people surfing around your site. Move them to the most interesting pages on your site or to your online store so they can buy.

At the end of every page, consider having some sort of link

to a different related page within your site. You don't want any dead end pages where the reader has no reason to keep looking at your site.

10. *Make Sure External Links Open in a "New Browser Window."* This is a biggie. External links are links to websites other than your own. If you list links to other websites that your visitors might be interested in (which is a great idea), be sure that when they click the link, a whole new browser window pops up. *Your site will stay open in a window underneath the new one.*

If the link doesn't open a new browser window, the other website appears in the same window where yours just was. Your website disappears. Bummer. You don't want visitors to leave your site for good, just to go check out another useful site.

11. *Avoid Pages with Little or No Content.* If you don't have anything to put on a page, take it off your site. A web page with just a single sentence or with "under construction" is annoying to your visitor. They want to be excited, entertained, informed, or interested by every page on the site.

12. *Give the Title Bar on Each Page a Good Name.* A small thing, but the details make the difference. The "title bar" is the bar at the very top of the Internet window. Have a title that describes the page. Something like "SuperScraps is Grand Haven's best store for scrapbook supplies" for a company information page. Or "Get a bouquet of roses from Fancy Florist and brighten her day" on a rose bouquet sales page. Too often these title bars just say "page 2" or "new product page." Ugh.

This is especially awful when you realize that the title bar is a big part of what search engines look at to decide if a page is relevant to a search request. Read more about this in New Customer Tactic #12: Get Good Search Engine Placement.

13. *Have Current Content—Frequently Updated.* Old information or long past events listed on your site take away from your credibility. If you don't have the newest information on your site, you're missing great marketing opportunities. Old and outdated information is frequently a problem if you have to go through your web developer to get any tiny thing changed on your site. Who has time (or money) for that?

There are websites that let you make all the changes you need to your site all by yourself—including adding and deleting pages—without knowing a single thing about web programming. More on that later in this section.

14. *Put Your E-Newsletter Sign-Up on Every Page.* Ask for the email addresses of every person who comes to your site and send them an e-newsletter, or do some other kind of email marketing. We believe that this is a tactic no retailer can do without. An entire section is devoted to email marketing later in this book. Your email sign-up box should be on every page of your website. Don't make visitors hunt around to get on your mailing list. Make it as easy as possible.

Whew! There you have it—14 points that will create a solid foundation when you're building your website. If your head is spinning and you wonder how you will ever accomplish all of that, don't worry. We can help.

After receiving too many horror stories from our clients about websites that cost too much and did too little, we decided to take matters into our own hands. We sat down and created a list of all the features a great website for a retail store would have, found a group of technical whizzes to put it together, and voila! We created WhizBang! Websites.

WhizBang! Websites are affordable, easy to build, you can change them yourself and most importantly, you get the step-by-step instructions we wrote especially for retailers like you on how to use your site to bring more money to your bottom line. To take a free, no obligation tour and see if a WhizBang! Website is the right choice for you, go to www.whizbangwebsites.com.

If you read those 14 points and feel great about your website, that is fantastic! Consider yourself among the lucky few.

Content Makes Your Website Great

If you've done all of the 14 things we suggested—have readable fonts, include contact information on every page, have links open a new browser section, have strong headlines, and so on—but have boring or irrelevant content, you won't have a great website.

> *To have a truly great website you must have information on your site that your customers need and want.*

To build a great website you must put yourself into your customers' shoes. You must think about your site from your customers' perspective. What are they hoping to find when they visit your site? Here are some suggestions.

Things They Need to Know: The Must-Haves   These elements are the bare minimum that your website should include. Make sure they are easy to find, easy to read, and customer-focused.

- *Your store phone number*—for all store locations if you have more than one.
- *Your street address*—for all store locations if you have more than one.
- *A map with a link to driving directions*—you can get this very easily from a variety of sources like Mapquest, Yahoo! Maps, or

Google Maps. Just copy and paste the code they provide from their site right onto yours.

- *Your store hours.*
- *A store email address.*
- *What merchandise you sell and what services you offer*—could include your basic product mix, your most popular brands. This information might be on one, several, or many pages on your site depending on your store.
- *Who you are and who your key staff people are*—with direct emails listed if at all possible. Remember, your relationships are your biggest competitive advantage. Make sure your customers can connect to you personally.
- *Information about your store*—a short history and branding statement.

Things They Want to Know: The Stuff That Makes Your Website Sizzle These elements are what make your site fun, interesting, important, and relevant for your customers. This is what will make you stand out from the crowd when a new customer checks you out for the first time and what will keep your current customers visiting over and over again. Here are just some of the possible elements you could include to make your site sizzle.

- *Information that positions you and your store as the expert.* Giving your customers good, interesting-to-them information is a key element in building a great website. This could be tips on how to use your product. Example: A vacuum store could list household cleaning tips, or a garden center could list planting tips.

    It could be articles written by you that are interesting for your customers. Example: A running store owner could write an article on the best 5-, 10-, and 15-mile runs in the area, or a coffee shop owner could write a page of recipes that use coffee as an ingredient.

It could be a list of your products with their best uses. Example: A fishing store lists the best baits for local fish in the past month, or an interior design store lists the top 10 trend colors for next year with the brand name paint color names that match.

- *Information about your special events and promotions.* Both before and especially *after* the event. Before the event, of course, give complete event details and an invitation to attend. If you have several events a year, have a schedule of events page. It is very important to keep this up-to-date.

  After the event post pictures, descriptions, contest results, anything fun or exciting that happened during your special event. Customers who were at the event as well as those who didn't attend will like going to this page.

- *Links to other resources.* Give them links to other noncompeting websites that they might find useful, interesting, or fun. Don't include links that aren't really relevant or are not very compelling—that will immediately shoot down your credibility and cool factor. It's better to have no links than bad ones. Don't forget to have these links open a new browser window. Otherwise your website will "disappear" when they click on the resource link.

- *A virtual store tour.* It's really true that a picture is worth a thousand words, and fortunately the Web is a very visual medium. Use as many pictures as possible to help your customers get a feel for your store, your products, and your services. It may sound too difficult to do, but it really can be quite easy. You don't need streaming video or audio. Simply take pictures of your store, give the pictures interesting captions, and put them in order on a page to create a "store tour."

- *Expanded information about you, your staff, and your store.* Anything you can do to enhance the human connection between you and your customers strengthens your competitive edge. A few possibilities: Include short bios with fun facts about each employee, employee product picks, a pictorial history of your store or company (my, you've aged gracefully!), or an Employee of the Month page.

There are so many more possibilities depending on the kind of business you have. Get creative. But I can guarantee you that if you use all five of the content suggestions just mentioned along with the eight must-have content pieces, you will have a website that will get you new customers and that your existing customers will love.

Help with Your Home Page

Probably the most difficult part of a website for any business owner to create is the home page. Having a really good one is important though, because it's the first look at your site that will make people decide to stay and click around or leave and surf right over to someone else's site.

What to say? What to say? First and foremost, always start with a great headline that grabs the visitor's attention. You'll read lots more on writing great headlines in the special section called Copywriting for Retailers.

After the headline, most people start writing a big block of text about what they know best—their store. From their own point of view. Yawn. The customer doesn't care. Yet. First, let them know what's inside the site—and your store—that's interesting or important for them.

Create a home page that shows them a little bit of what you've got and invites them in for more. Put several snippets of information with links to the pages inside your site where your visitor can learn more. It may help to think of your home page as an abbreviated table of contents or as a launching pad that can take your website visitor to the place that's best for them.

Choose items that many visitors will need: *Get a Map to the Store Nearest You.*

Choose items that you want to direct lots of people to see: *Preorder the Hottest Items from the International Trade Fair Expo—Before They Sell Out!*

Choose items that have high interest value for your visitors: *Spring Gardening Checklist: 12 Things Your Garden Needs Right Now.*

Choose items that hold a lot of intrigue value that will encourage people to click: *What's in a Moose Poop Sundae? Click here to find out.*

You can put your information items on your home page as short blocks of *text*, as *button* images, or with *pictures*. And you can use them in combination together. One is not necessarily better than another; it just depends on your website design and general layout. See Figure 1.5 for an example of each style

Each one of these styles does its job: letting customers know about the flower of the month and getting them to click into the site to learn more about tulips or see the special tulip bouquets.

If you can create a website that has a solid foundation, an interesting home page, and lots of great content, you will have an amazing tool for attracting new customers and, as you'll read later in the book, a wonderful way to connect with your existing customers.

Flower of the Month: Tulip

Tulips are a sure sign of spring and have a fascinating history to boot. Learn more about the Dutch tulip trade and check out how we've used the tulip in five special spring bouquets.

Flower of the Month

Tulip

Tulips are a sure sign of spring and have a fascinating history to boot. Learn more about the Dutch tulip trade and check out how we've used the tulip in five special spring bouquets.

Flower of the Month

TULIP

A sure sign of spring, tulips have a fascinating history. Check out how we've used the tulip in five special spring bouquets.

Figure 1.5   Information Items on a Home Page: Text Block, Button Image, or Picture.

Whether it's a simple electronic brochure for your store or a full-blown e-commerce site, a great website is an absolutely essential tool for independent store owners in the twenty-first century.

New Customer Tactic #8: Seek Out Reciprocal Links

The next three tactics to get new customers are high-tech variations on the affinity marketing techniques we explored in the previous section. Look for others who have contact with people you'd like to get as customers and ask for an endorsement.

In this tactic look for other websites that your customers may visit and see if their owners will put an external link from their site to yours. In other words, you want them to list you on their resource page. The first place to go looking for these websites is any resource site that you are linking to from your own site.

In many cases this will work extremely well. For example, if you own a camera and photography store and you link to a local custom framing gallery that you recommend to your customers, it would be natural for the framing gallery to link back to your site. This is a great combination of both affinity marketing and the rule of reciprocity in action. You scratch their back, they'll scratch yours, and the customer wins both ways.

In some cases a website you list as a resource for your customers may not be a good fit to link back to your site. For example, if you're an outdoor outfitter specializing in fishing, you may want to link to your state fishing regulations website. While you might like them to link back to you—they won't! The government just will not endorse your website.

Here's another situation where your resources link may not work as a reciprocal link. Unless you have an e-commerce website, it's not very useful to have a site from another state or a national website link back to you. For example, if you own a musical instrument store a link to the Rock and Roll Hall of Fame would be a cool resource for your customers, but having them link back to your site probably wouldn't do any good unless you had online selling capabilities. Most of their site visitors would simply be located too far from your store to do any good.

The second place to look for other sites that would be willing to link back to yours is any of the nonprofit organizations you are partnering with and donating money to. Ask if they will put a link on their website to yours so their members can easily visit and buy.

Also ask your local chamber of commerce, visitors bureau, convention bureau, and downtown organization websites if they will link to yours. You may need to be a member of the group for them to link their site to yours, but if the match is close enough it may be a good investment for you. Some of them will not require that you are a member; they want to provide good information for their site visitors, too.

Next, go back to that list you made of affinity businesses. Some of them may be great candidates for this kind of reciprocal link. Maybe some weren't interested in doing an endorsed mailing with you but would love to swap links. This works especially well for closely aligned, but not overlapping, businesses. A sewing shop linking to a yarn store makes excellent sense, for example. It's highly likely that they share customers even though they don't share a lot of the same merchandise.

Last, open your mind and really think about all the possibilities—sites that you might not list as a resource for your customers, but who could easily endorse you to theirs. For example, if the yarn store just mentioned had a prayer shawl knitting night, they might try to get a link on every church website in the city as well as on any sites of religious bookstores, religious charities, or other women's groups. I think prayer shawl night would be full—and so would the cash register.

Just as with the other affinity marketing tactics, one of the big keys to making this one successful is to make it easy for your partner to link to you. Give them web copy for a text link, maybe the

HTML code they need to do a button style link, and of course, the URL of exactly the page you want them to send their customers to. Maybe this is your home page, maybe it's your online shopping cart, maybe it is another page of special interest to the group in question. Don't make your partner figure it out. Do all the work for them so there's no reason for them *not* to do it and every reason *to* do it.

New Customer Tactic #9: Set Up Email Endorsements

This tactic is the high-tech version of New Customer Tactic #2: Send an Endorsed Mailing and it works *exactly the same way*, except that you have to partner with a business that's sending e-newsletters or another kind of email marketing message to their customers. This may be a little bit tricky and may limit the number of potential partners you have because not nearly enough businesses are taking advantage of this amazing marketing tactic. Read more on email marketing in Step Three: Get Your Customers to Shop More Often.

Hot Tip!

Sometimes a link you'd like to include in an email is just too long or cumbersome to work well. Long links can get broken in an email and the reader then has to cut and paste it into a browser rather than just click on it. Sometimes the link is confusing for the reader.

There are lots of free services that allow you to create a short link from a long one. Change this: http://www.whizbangtraining .com/cart/#Mega-Packs:%20Buy%20More%20and%20Save Into this: http://snipurl.com/megapack.

Check out the Retailer Resources page on our website for a list of the best of these free services.

Once you've found a suitable partner, ask them to endorse your store in one of their email blasts. With email, you can get new customers into your store two different ways:

1. *Have your partner include a "virtual" gift certificate for your store:* "This $5 Gift Certificate to Wally's Widgets is my way of celebrating our 23rd year in business. Thank you for being such a wonderful customer! Just print out this email with the gift certificate and take it in to Wally's for $5 off your favorite Widget."

2. *Have them include a link to your website*—either to your home page, a shopping cart page, or to a page of special interest to their customers. By including a link to your website you make it supereasy for your partner's customers to check you out. They don't have to go to your physical store; they can immediately click and see what you have to offer them.

Of course, if you can get your partner to both include a gift certificate and link to your website, you're that much further ahead!

The key thing is to do all the work for your partner business. Write out exactly what you want them to include in their email blast. That way all they have to do is cut and paste it into their message. Remember: It has to sound like it's coming from your partner, not from you. You'll have more people willing to partner with you if you make it easy, and you'll also have more control over what gets said about your business.

The benefits to your partner business are exactly the same as in sending an endorsed mailing via snail mail. They get to give their customers something of value and therefore increase the personal relationship they have with their customers. Think about it. Whom do you give gifts to? People you like and care about. That's what they want their customers to know—that they like and care about them.

The benefits to the customer are exactly the same as in the low-tech tactic. They get something free. A gift certificate to your store. The benefits to you, however, are increased. You get to drive visitors to your website as well as into your store. Plus, sending email is easier, cheaper, and faster than doing a snail mail endorsed mailing. Lots easier. Lots cheaper. Lots faster.

New Customer Tactic #10: Ask Customers to Forward to a Friend

Because forwarding an email message is so easy, it's a great way to get new customer referrals. Just as with the low-tech version of getting new customers through referrals the key is to *ask*. You can't just hope they'll pass your emails along; you have to be proactive. Always ask your customers to forward your email newsletter to friends and family who might find them interesting or useful.

A Very Important Point   When you are asking your readers to forward your message to their friends, you must be very clear about what you want their friends to do. The only thing you want the people who receive the forward to do is *sign up for your email newsletter*. Don't try to get them to come into your store (some will and that's great), don't try to sell them something online, don't try to get them to do anything but sign up for your email newsletter.

Once you have their email address and they're getting your regular e-marketing, *then* you can try to get them into your store, or sell them something online, or whatever else you can think of.

Make the forward to a friend request part of your email "template"—the format you use each time you send your newsletter. Most of the time you'll want to put this referral request at the end of your email message. After your customer has read the email and has enjoyed the information you've provided or is excited about what's happening at your store, that's the time to strike! They may already be thinking, "Gee, Phil should know about this." See Figure 1.6 for some possible language.

If you have a longer email message—more like a newsletter with several sections or articles—you could very effectively put your referral request in the middle of the email in between two of your best sections. The idea is to ask them to forward when they like what they're reading and will feel good about sending it on to a friend.

We know one guy with a monthly newsletter who puts "Pls. Forward to a Friend" at the end of every one of his subject lines. We're not 100 percent sold on this idea, but it may work for you depending on your business. My feeling is that you want the subject line to make the recipient *open* the email, not forward it along. Must be working for him though, because he's a smart guy and he's still doing it.

Asking your customers to forward your emails is simple to do

Know other people that might enjoy getting the *Gardening Gazette*? Please forward this edition and encourage them to sign up by clicking the link below.

	Note: If you have a good email program like WhizBang! Email this subscribe link will sign them up automatically with no extra work on your part!
<paste subscribe link here>	

Or have them send me an email at yourname@youremail.com and write Sign Me Up in the subject line.

Figure 1.6 **Sample Referral Request.**

and could get you lots of new customers with very little work and virtually no expense on your part. If you are really good, lucky, or both, your email messages will become "viral." You know how a real virus spreads—one person has a germ, sneezes, spreads the germs to lots of other people, and infects them. Then they start sneezing and pass it along to many others and pretty soon *everyone* is infected.

Same thing happens with emails because it is so easy to forward a message to many people at once. I'm sure you know exactly what we're talking about; it's that email that gets forwarded to you from multiple friends who don't even know each other.

Email messages that are very interesting, funny, or have a lot of valuable information have a much greater chance of being forwarded to lots of friends. Having a "forward this to a friend" request is important, but creating an email that is so good people *want* to send it to lots of other people is better.

New Customer Tactic #11: Online User Groups and Chat Rooms

Another great way to leverage the power of "viral marketing" is through online user groups and chat rooms. This tactic works extremely well for the kind of stores that market to customers who are likely to enjoy talking to each other:

- Hobby based stores—bike stores, music stores, boating stores, knitting stores, scrapbooking stores, sewing stores, camera stores, model shops, garden centers, to name just a few.
- Stores whose customers are passionate about the product or service—religious bookstores, children's stores, health food stores, or art galleries for example.

Whenever you have a place where large groups of highly targeted potential customers gather, you have a great opportunity to get your message out. In the case of online chat rooms or user groups, you have a couple of options for promoting your business.

Some chat rooms or user groups will offer ad space that you can buy. It may be expensive however, so beware. Another way to use a user group or chat room to your advantage is to join the group and offer yourself as an expert voice. You can do this in much the same way that you position yourself as the expert on your website: You can give tips, create checklists, explain advanced techniques, offer advice, start discussions, or suggest additional resources. What you usually can't do is make blatantly promotional pitches; the moderators of the site will probably kick you out. If you want to participate directly in the group you will have to be much more subtle about your marketing to the other participants. But that doesn't mean it can't be effective.

Probably the best, most powerful way to get new customers from a chat room or user group is to have one of your current customers—who is already a participant in the group—sing your praises and recommend you, your products, and your services. It's word-of-mouth advertising in cyber-space!

Go ahead and *ask* your customers if they will do this. It's just like asking for a referral or asking them to forward your email to a friend. Hoping that they will mention you on their favorite chat group doesn't cut it.

What you should *not* do is join a group and pose as someone else or pretend to be a customer recommending your store. This is just plain lying. There are so many wonderful, ethical ways to promote your business that you don't need to do this. Remember: What you give out to the world, you'll get back. If you treat your prospects with respect and integrity you'll get back great lifelong customers. If you treat them dishonestly, you'll get angry people who will never be your customers.

New Customer Tactic #12: Get Good Search Engine Placement

For strictly online businesses this topic is of utmost importance, and entire books can and have been written about the subject. For most retail store owners what we cover here is more than enough.

Remember: Your website won't magically make you competitive with Amazon.com or any of the other big boys in your industry. Your website is a tool for you to use with your current customers and hottest local prospects. For most of you, having great content on your site is a lot more important than having great search engine ranking. But once you've built a wonderful website, you definitely want to make sure your customers and hottest prospects can find it easily.

Make sure that your website comes up on the first page of search results if someone searches on *the name of your store*, or searches on *your main product with your city name and/or ZIP code*. That's it.

To get good search engine placement in this context takes two steps and is not too difficult. First, make your website friendly for the search engines and second, submit the URL (the domain address) of your website to the search engines.

Make Your Website Search Engine Friendly

In order for your site to get search results, first, make it easy for the search engine to find and "read" you. The main idea here is to include the words and phrases that your customers might be searching for in three specific parts of your website.

The Title Bar   In the section called 14 Points to Consider When Building Your Website we mentioned that you need to have good title bars for every page of your website. On a PC platform computer, the title bar is at the very top of the browser. The title bar is usually blue with white letters and says something about the website you're looking at and then gives the name of the web browser you're using: Microsoft Internet Explorer, Netscape, or others. On a Mac platform the title bar is in the center of the window right above the address bar. It is usually grey with black letters.

Your title bar should read like a sentence or phrase and include words that your customers might be searching on. Unfortunately all too often they say something awful like "index," "home page," or "product #2857736." Not at all friendly to search engines or human beings!

For the home page of a scrapbook supply store this would be a good title bar:

SuperScraps is Grand Haven's best store for scrapbook supplies

It would generate results for a number of different searches that a customer might possibly do including the store name, Super-Scraps, and the product/location combination "scrapbook store Grand Haven." It would also give results in searches for "scrapbook supplies Grand Haven" or "SuperScraps Grand Haven."

This kind of title has lots of key words that customers might be searching for, and it also reads like a real sentence or phrase that gives the human user information.

Give each page of your website a good title bar. Many of them may be the same, but if you have pages about specific things, you may want to write a title bar that gives more information.

For a page on a florist's website describing rose bouquets a good title bar might be:

Get a bouquet of roses from Fancy Florist
in Tacoma, Washington and brighten her day

This title would yield search results for many different combinations of words that your customer might be searching on including the store name, city, roses, bouquet. So someone searching on "roses Tacoma, WA" would get the Fancy Florist website as one of their search results.

We think getting a good title bar is really important, so that's why we made it so easy to do when you use WhizBang! Websites. You can give every page the title bar *you* want it to have and can change it whenever you want to with no waiting, paying, or fussing.

If you are using a web developer, be sure to tell them *specifically* what you want the title bar to say for each page of your website. Do *not* count on them to create an appropriate title bar for you. Most of these folks are not marketers and don't know much about your business or understand your prospects. You do.

Home Page Content   Just like your title bar, the search engines are "reading" the content of your home page and looking for the words or phrases your customers are searching for, so try to incorporate those words and phrases into your home page copy.

The closer to the exact phrase, the better the search result. For example, if someone were searching for our company name "WhizBang! Training," websites that have the two words whizbang and training right next to each other will give better results than pages that contain both of the words, but are not next to each other.

In other words, you might find a website that has the sentence, "The boy had a *whizbang* idea for *training* dogs without using a leash." in the search results for WhizBang! Training, but it would be ranked lower than our company site because it doesn't have the exact phrase being searched for.

So one of the tricks to getting new customers through good search engine placement is to guess which words and phrases your hot prospects are most likely to be searching for and use them in your home page copy.

This is one reason you should have your store name and contact information on every page of your site. It will help you out in searches that include your city name, your state, or your ZIP code.

Warning: Please do not write silly-sounding, contorted copy for your home page trying to get in every possible combination of words and phrases your customers might be searching on. This is counterproductive. The most important thing to do when writing the copy for your home page is to make it interesting, inviting, and relevant to your *human* customers, not the search engines. But if you can do both—great!

Meta-Tags   What the heck is a meta-tag? They are lists of key words associated with a page on your website that are invisible to your site visitors, but can be "read" by the search engines. Each page can have its own meta-tag list.

Create meta-tag lists that include the possible variations, different spellings, misspellings, jargon, or colloquialisms that your hot prospects might use when they are searching. For example, a tanning salon might want to include these words, among others, in a meta-tag list:

> tan, tans, tanning, tanning salon, tanning salons,
> tanning bed, tanning beds, taning, suntan, suntans, sun tan,
> sun tanning, suntanning, spray tanning, tanning booth,
> sunscreen, tanning accelerator, tanning lotion,
> suntan lotion, UV rays, UVA rays, UVB rays, sun

Just as with the title bar, you can use the same meta-tag list for every page of your site, or you can tailor the list to reflect the specific information on that page. If you're using WhizBang! Websites, it's extremely easy to create, change, or update your meta-tag list on every page of your site by yourself. If you're using a web developer, create the meta-tag lists and tell them which lists to attach to which pages in your site. Again, don't count on them to create this list for you.

Submit Your Site to the Search Engines

Now that you have made your website search engine friendly, you have to submit it. Tell them that your website exists. If you don't do this, the bot crawlers and web spiders may eventually find you, but they may not. You're safer submitting your site than simply hoping it will be found. (You remember "hope marketing," don't you?)

Now this next part of the equation is a little bit tricky because things in the search engine world are changing constantly and rapidly. Unlike the rest of the information in this book, what we suggest today may not be the best advice tomorrow—let alone five years from now. So we just have to take our best shot at this with the caveat that you should check our website for any changes that have taken place in the world since the writing of this book.

Google   Google is far and away the dominant search engine on the Internet.

Pretty much everyone else is keying their search results from Google—including Yahoo!, MSN, and AOL.

With this in mind, our #1 recommendation is that you submit your website for *free* to Google here: www.google.com/addurl.

You only have to submit the main domain URL for your website (www.yourdomain.com) and then let the Googlebot do the rest. It will "crawl" around your site learning about it and storing information for when a prospect searches for something that may match your site.

The down side to this free submitting tactic is that it may take some time—up to a month or more—for Google to register your site and have it show up on search results.

Once your site has been registered with Google, it will get picked up by all the other search engines as their crawlers go out into the Web and look for what's out there. It may take several more months for your site to be found by all the major search engines. This may sound like too long to you, but keep in mind that this is all completely free and basically takes no effort on your part.

If you want to get noticed in cyber-space right away, you may want to check out the Google AdWords campaigns. You have to pay for these ads, but you can target them to just the people who are searching in your selling area. This means that if someone lives in Detroit and searches for a tanning salon and you have a tanning salon in Detroit, the Google ad for your salon will come up, but if your tanning salon is in Minneapolis, it won't.

As with any other advertising, the more targeted you can be, the more profitable your investment will be. So if you're really interested in using your website to get lots of new customers, buying targeted Google AdWords may be right for you.

Other Ways to Submit Your Website

There are *tons* of services out there promising to submit your site for free to 10, 15, 30, or more search engines. Usually the only one of any size or importance in the free submission list is Google, and you can do that one yourself for free in about two minutes without giving out your contact info to anybody. If you do use one of these services, be prepared to be hounded mercilessly to upgrade to their paid submission services.

If you agree to pay for their submission services, they will usually submit your site to the other bigger search engines like Yahoo!, MSN, AOL, AltaVista, Excite, Dogpile, Lycos, and others. Of course, all these search engines will automatically pick you up from your Google listing in a few months anyway.

Be very careful of any service that promises they can "guarantee" you a top search ranking. No one can promise that—the search algorithms are far too complicated, changeable, and secret for anyone to promise you that. It's just a scam and a sign of questionable ethics.

In addition, lots of these services will try to sell you "search engine optimization," or SEO. This just means that they will check your title bars, home page content, and meta-tags to make sure they are search engine friendly. If you follow the process we've outlined previously, you won't need this. The fact is that you know your business, your customers, prospects, and website much better than they ever could. So armed with some basic information, you can probably make a better title bar or meta-tag list than one of these services.

Bottom line: Unless you are in a really big hurry to get your website listed, you may just want to do the free Google submission and call it a day. It's slow but sure—and you can't beat the price!

The Traditional Media

Why Advertising Doesn't Usually Work for Independent Retailers and What You Can Do About It

You may have the impression from earlier in the book that we don't like traditional advertising. And it's true; we're not big fans of traditional advertising for most small retail and service businesses. Here's why:

- Traditional advertising is expensive and most small businesses don't have the resources to do it correctly.
- Most small business owners don't know how to advertise correctly—so it *doesn't work*.

An expensive tactic that doesn't work. Not really our cup of tea. And so for most of you, the best advice is *not* to do much, if any, traditional advertising.

However, you should know a little bit more about how and when advertising does work and when and why it doesn't. That way you can make informed decisions when the sales rep from your local newspaper or cable station comes around. My first word of caution is about those sales reps. Far too many of these well-meaning people don't know the first thing about marketing a small business.

What they do know how to do is sell ad space. Same thing goes for the graphic designer from your local newspaper or yellow pages. They can use the software design program, but that doesn't mean that they know how to design ads that are effective at selling your merchandise.

There are some exceptions, but *you* have to know the difference between a good, effective ad campaign and a bad one. Don't expect to get expert advice from most of these people. So here goes—our rules of the road for advertising.

Selling Your Business versus Selling a Product

There are two basic types of advertising campaigns, and many people get them confused. The first is an image campaign, which creates name recognition—sometimes called top-of-mind-awareness. The second is a product or event ad campaign.

In the first type of campaign, what you're really selling is your business. You're trying to educate the public about what you do and why they should shop with you. To be successful at this kind of advertising you *must* have one important element:

Repetition.

You have to run a consistent looking ad (or group of ads) with a consistent (benefit) message over and over for a long period of time. It's best if you do it in a variety of media (newspaper, radio, etc.) so people get the message in many different forms from many different sources. It really should be a coordinated, planned effort not just a scattershot approach. By the time you're absolutely sick of your ads, the general public will just be noticing them.

I know what you're thinking. This sounds really expensive. Yeah, it can be. But if you use image type ads only once or twice and expect a flood of people to come rushing into your store checking you out, you're bound to be disappointed. So don't waste the money.

That's why this type of advertising is best left to larger companies who can devote many, many thousands of dollars to it. And
some of you with multiple locations and big annual sales could
probably do some of this (we did at the Mackinaw Kite Co.), but
you should do it as an *addition* to the other lower-cost, highly effective tactics we cover in this book, not as a first marketing effort.

In the second kind of ad campaign, your ads should not sell your
business, but a product or service you offer or a special event you are
having—like a clearance sale. This kind of product or event focused
ad can be run for much shorter periods of time but should still be re-
peated as close together and as often as you can afford.

For example, if you're having a clearance sale, run the biggest
ad you can afford every day for a week before the sale. If you're trying to sell the new Ultra 5000 Aqua Widget during the holidays,
run ads three times a week for the whole month of December.

Here are two very sketchy examples of both kinds of ads. Can
you tell which is which?

Great Gifts For Kids . . . **And Fun Grown-Ups!** **The Mackinaw Kite Co.** **(logo)** **Where FUN Begins** Address, Phone, Web, Hours	**Yo-Yo Fun for Everyone!** **The Brain Yo-Yo** Makes an amazing stocking stuffer for beginning and experienced yo-yo players alike. $14.99 Mackinaw Kite Co. Address, Phone, Web, Hours

Picking the Right Advertising Media

One important component of doing advertising correctly is to pick
the right media to use. One type of advertising might work well for
some businesses or some applications, but not for others.

When choosing the media for your advertising efforts, be very aware of their geographic "reach." For example, if you live in a small suburb of a larger city, you would probably be better off advertising in a small local newspaper with a small readership than with the bigger metro newspaper with a big readership. This is because most people tend to shop within five miles of their homes. Why pay for readers who probably will never make the trip to shop with you?

In fact, if you advertise too far out of your geographic area, you could very well end up generating business for your competition. We know a chiropractor who loves it when a nearby (but not local) practice advertises in the paper. She swears her appointments start picking up whenever the other practice advertises. His ads remind readers that, yeah, their back does ache—but the other practice is too far away and so they call her!

This concept of geographic reach is also very true of billboard advertising. If you're going to buy a billboard or two, they had better be very near your store.

Best Homemade Ice Cream on the Lakeshore

Turn left NOW to Ike's Ice-Cream-O-Rama

Another important element to consider when you are choosing where to advertise is how "targeted" the media is on your potential customers. For example, a children's furniture store might opt to place ads in the *El Paso Family Magazine* and forget about buying space in the *El Paso Times*. Or a religious bookstore might buy newspaper ads to run only on Saturdays on the same page as the church listings.

If you're in a small town, radio spots on the local station that plays in every office and restaurant might be worthwhile. It's very targeted on your specific market. Regional radio spots on a bigger station might not work as well.

Once again, precision = profit.

Other Types of Advertising Tools

High impact, low-cost advertising involves buying ads in small publications, such as the newsletters of local groups, programs for local events, and magazines catering to small, highly specific groups of hobbyists or people with a particular interest.

Examples of places to find high impact, low-cost advertising opportunities are:

- The program for your local high school holiday pageant.
- Place mats at local hangout restaurants.
- The program for any amateur sports tournament.
- Community festivals, parades, special events.
- The program for your local community theater, symphony, or museum.
- Senior citizens fairs, festivals, and other activities.

Most of these organizations are strapped for cash and any help you can give to offset the cost of printing is rewarded with genuine gratitude. The kind of gratitude that translates into business.

You'll find that you can buy an ad in many of these publications for as little as $20, and if you pick the right organizations, your ads will reach your targeted groups and hottest prospects.

City Maps and Chamber Brochures

These can be effective if you have a business that's interesting to visitors to your town, like an ice cream store, hotel, restaurant, an "attraction" business, or sells something that could be a souvenir. This kind of ad can also work if you have a general interest business that's located in a high-traffic visitor shopping destination, like a downtown art gallery or home gift store.

But if your main customer base is locals and visitors are unlikely to purchase your product or services (flowers, vacuums, hearing aids, and so forth), don't bother. Likewise if your store location is too far from the main visitor destinations, forget it.

Yellow Pages

Everyone should have a listing in the yellow pages, but not everyone needs a display ad. These display ads are really expensive and, as we said earlier, the Internet is consistently cutting into the effectiveness of hard-copy books. It's not hard to understand why. You can learn so much more about a business by browsing around its website than by reading an ad in the yellow pages book—no matter how big the ad is.

But since there are still people out there using the book (and probably will be in the near future), this kind of advertising remains important. The single most frequently asked question we get about yellow pages ads is, "How big should my ad be?" Not surprising, since increasing the size of your ad significantly increases the cost of your ad.

The real question is, "Does a big ad bring big results? Big enough to be worth the extra dough?"

There's no question: Statistics show that *in general*, bigger ads result in more calls. But does that mean that a huge ad is right for your business?

Not necessarily. If you're in an industry with lots of competition in your market area, a big ad might be just what you need. Think pizza joints, insurance companies, florists, beauty salons, and the like. Or if you're in the kind of business where people go to the yellow pages to find you for the first time (usually because they need you *right now*) a big ad can attract attention. Plumber, anyone?

But if you're the only health food store in town, you don't need to buy a half page ad, no matter what the yellow pages sales guy tells you! And if you just can't afford a big ad—even if you're in one of those categories just mentioned—you shouldn't buy one. In fact, what's written in your ad may be even more important than the size of the ad anyway.

If you do spend the money for a display ad, be sure that it's an ad that works to get you the phone call, not just an expensive version of your business card. Here's the number one thing to avoid if you want a good ad in the yellow pages: Do *not* let the art department at the phone book company create your ad.

I know that the yellow pages salesperson is going to be pushing this; it makes your decision easier, and therefore makes their sale easier. But it will absolutely make your ad worse. Why? Why is it such a bad idea to have someone else create your ad for free? Sounds like it could be a good deal.

Reason #1   The person at the phone book company is more than likely just someone off the street who knows how to use a graphic design program—a techie with an interest in art. If you're somewhat lucky, you'll at least get a trained graphic designer. But how many really good graphic designers do you think are sticking around a job doing yellow pages ads?

Even if you get a trained designer, they are rarely—if ever—a marketing professional. They might know design, but they don't know marketing. And that's the perfect recipe for a potentially pretty—but highly ineffective—ad. In other words, a waste of your money.

Reason #2   The person at the phone book company doesn't know about *your* business. Yeah, sure, they may know what a florist does, or a framer does, or what a sewing shop sells, but they don't know what makes you special. Only you know that.

Hot Tip!

One of our most highly recommended resources is a downloadable e-book that explains exactly how to create a yellow pages ad that works. It's packed with more than 90 pages of great information written by a guy who's an expert in this one particular style of advertising. A real gold mine!

If you do any yellow page display ads, you should read this book. It gets our absolute top rating as a business resource and is well worth every penny.

Check it out on the Retailer Resources page of our website, www.whizbangtraining.com.

Reason #3   If the person who does your ad is the same person who creates 1,538 other ads in the book, what chance do you think you have of looking different? Of standing out? Pretty slim.

To get a great yellow pages ad that's worth the astronomical amounts of money they charge, you have to create your own ad.

Now I don't mean that you have to be the graphic designer, but you must decide exactly what you want your ad to say, in what order you want your ad copy to be placed, and precisely how all the different elements should work together. If you can't do this, don't bother spending the money on a big yellow pages ad.

For All Your Advertising Efforts

If you choose to do any kind of traditional advertising, please remember this one thing if you don't remember anything else from this section:

Copy is King!

What you say in your ad and how you say it are vitally important—probably much more important than what the ad looks like, how big it is, or where you've placed it. In fact you can have good-looking, big ads all over the place in great media locations, but if the ad copy is bad you're just wasting your money.

This is not just true of advertising, but really for *all* of your marketing efforts. Letters, postcards, bag stuffers, emails, websites, brochures, event flyers, everything you do!

That's why we've included the next section, Copywriting for Retailers. You simply can't have great advertising or marketing without great copy.

Don't misunderstand, however. We're not recommending yucky looking ads. If you're going to spend the money to advertise, get a good graphic designer to lay out your ads for you so they look professional and polished. This is your face to the world and just as you wouldn't leave the house with spinach stuck in your teeth, you shouldn't put a sloppy business face to the world.

If you learn the Ten Commandments of Copywriting for Retailers, use a competent graphic designer, and choose the right kind of medium for your business, you will never again create a lame, boring, money-sucking advertisement.

SPECIAL SECTION

Copywriting for Retailers

Killer Copy: How to Write Messages That Sell

In its essence great marketing is simple. To persuade people to purchase from you, all you have to do is

Get The *Right Message*.
To The *Right Person*.
Using The *Right Tactic*.
At The *Right Time*.

If you can get the right mix of those four components, you've got a surefire sale.

But most people focus only on one part of this powerful four-way equation—the tactic. Whether it's a brochure, a special event, a customer newsletter, or a radio spot, people spend most of their time thinking about what kind of marketing tactic to use.

Don't get me wrong; Using the right tools, or methods, for your business *is* very important. But you can create as many brochures, or special events, or newspaper ads, or direct mail pieces as you want, and if they don't deliver a *compelling message* about why someone should try your store, product, or service, it just won't matter.

This is precisely why most small business owners rarely find traditional print advertising (newspaper, yellow pages, etc.) effective: They don't know how to write ad copy that sells. The method is fine; it's the message that falls flat.

That's why we include this special section on Copywriting for Retailers: to help you learn how to create a compelling message for your marketing efforts.

If you have any doubts about how important it really is to focus on the copywriting part of the four-part equation—on focusing and crafting the words in your message—let me state right here, unequivocally, that it is *Really, Really Important!*

Without a well-written, precisely crafted message, none of your marketing efforts will be as powerful and effective as you want them to be—*need* them to be.

In fact, great copywriting is so important that people do it for a living, and the best ones get paid big, *big* bucks to do it. I'm talking private yacht, apartment in Paris, never-worry-about-money-again kind of bucks. In fact, we personally know a guy who pulled in more than $400k last year writing copy *part-time.*

Why do they get paid so much? Because great copy is what *sells.* Now, I'm not suggesting that you need to become a master copywriter, but I do think that *you must learn copywriting basics to be an effective marketer.*

Working On Your Message

To start, understand why customers should shop with you and be able to express this clearly and succinctly. In essence, you must discover what you really sell. It's the foundation of all your marketing messages.

When I owned the Mackinaw Kite Co., I didn't sell kites and toys; I sold *fun.* As a matter of fact our tag line was Where FUN Begins.

When you start to get down to the deep emotional benefits of your product, service, or store, then you'll realize what you really sell. So go ahead and think about why someone should shop with you. You may want to spend a few minutes jotting some of those reasons down right now. Make as big a list as you can.

If you're like 99 percent of the clients we work with, you now have a list of features that describe your store and your products. It's a good start, but to create killer copy that increases sales, you must go deeper.

Features versus Benefits

One of the biggest problems people have when they create marketing materials is that they focus on features and largely ignore *benefits*. A feature describes what a product or service has; a benefit describes how a product solves a problem, or better yet how it will make someone feel. Both are important, but when you're creating marketing messages, always *start* by talking about the benefits, and then follow up and support your claim by explaining the features.

You could go on and on about what great stuff you sell and what a great store you have, but unless you turn the features into compelling benefits, your customers and prospects are going to say a big "So What?"

Here are some examples that will help you as you turn your store, product, or service features into benefits:

Product/Service:	Apple iPod.
Feature:	20 mb hard drive.
Benefit:	Holds 5,000 songs.
Deeper Benefit:	Never be without any of your favorite music.

Product/Service:	Frying pan.
Feature:	Teflon coating.
Benefit:	Food won't stick to the pan.
Deeper Benefit	Supereasy, incredibly quick cleanup.

Product/Service: Hearing aid.
Feature: Digital technology.
Benefit: Clearer, more realistic sound.
Deeper Benefit: Being able to have a conversation with your grandchildren around a crowded Thanksgiving dinner table.

Product/Service: Flowers.
Feature: Fresh.
Benefit: More attractive, wonderful smell, last longer.
Deeper Benefit: Giving the best shows your love, appreciation, good taste.

Product/Service: Marketing Mentor Program.
Feature: Personalized coaching.
Benefit: Better marketing plan resulting in more sales and profits.
Deeper Benefit: Feeling confident in your long-term ability to create the business of your dreams.

Product/Service: Home accessories.
Feature: Contemporary styling.
Benefit: A home that has a sophisticated, "magazine quality" feel.
Deeper Benefit: Feeling proud of and comfortable in your home.

Terrific Tip: The more you can tap into feelings, the more effective your marketing will be. Why? Because people *buy on emotion* (desire, fear, envy, joy) and *justify the purchase with logic*.

To create truly great marketing pieces, understand or create precise, compelling emotional benefits for your customers and prospects and then communicate them clearly. Tell them exactly *what's in it for them* when they buy from you.

Okay, now take the list you wrote of why someone should shop with you, and switch anything you wrote that is a feature of your store or the products you sell into a benefit for the customer. Make yourself a new list that's full of customer benefits.

Another really good—and eye-opening—exercise for you to do is to take any of your existing marketing materials like a brochure, or an event flyer, or a printout of your home page and mark all the words that describe features in blue highlighter and all the words that describe benefits in yellow highlighter. Have a blue page full of features? Don't despair, almost everyone else does, too. But if you can change those features into benefits, you'll attract the attention of your hot prospects and current customers.

Make the Big Switch

The second part of creating a message that sells involves switching your marketing language to focus on your *customer*, not on *you*. Never forget: Your customer does not care about you or your business; they care only about how well you are meeting their needs. I know it sounds harsh, but it's true.

So when you speak to them, write a letter to them, or create a brochure for them, make the focus *them*, not *you*. This means going through all of your marketing materials and looking for opportunities to change *I/me/my/we/our* in the copy to *you/yours*, especially at the beginnings of your sentences, and especially in your headlines! *Please note that using your store name is equivalent to saying we or I.*

Here are several examples that take *we* focused messages filled with features and switch them to *you* focused messages filled with benefits.

Before: "We sell only the healthiest plants."
After: "Your plants will look better and live longer when they
           come from XYZ Garden Center."

Before: "At Gertrude's Shoes, we offer a 100% money-back
           guarantee." (This is a double whammy, putting both the
           store name and the *we* in front.)
After: "You take absolutely no risk when you buy from us. Your
           satisfaction is 100% guaranteed."

Before: "We've been in business since 1959."
After: "You can trust our 45 years of experience."

Before: "Our carpet extraction process eliminates odors."
After: "Your carpet will smell fresher than you ever thought
           possible—thanks to our patented odor extraction
           system."

Please notice that in all of these statements I actually do talk about
the products, service, or store. It's just that the primary focus of the
statement is on the customer and highlights a customer benefit. *It's
the big switch.*

This brings us neatly to headlines.

Headlines

Every piece of marketing material you create *must have a headline*. I
can't state it strongly enough. Whether it's a postcard, a letter, a
display ad, a TV commercial, a classified ad, a brochure, website, an
in-store sign, a billboard (which is nothing *but* a headline, really), a
radio ad, or an email, it should have a headline.

Here's why. You must give your reader/listener/looker a reason to keep on reading, or listening, or looking at the rest of your message.

Email is a great example. The subject line of an email is the headline of your message. Write a good headline, and the recipient is likely to open the email and keep reading. A bad, boring, or non-existent subject line: Well, what do you do with those messages? Most people delete them.

In fact, the headline is the *most important piece of copywriting* for any marketing materials you create. A good headline can increase customer response by 100 percent, 500 percent, even 1,000 percent! That's the difference between a marketing effort that's wildly successful and one that's a total bust.

Here's the *number one headline mistake* most people make when creating marketing materials: They put their company name and/or logo at the top of the page where the headline should go. This may come as a crushing blow, but your store name or logo just isn't enough incentive for people to keep reading. In your headline, make the customer feel the *benefit* of owning your product, or using your services, or attending your promotion. The feeling a good headline creates makes them want to read more.

The headline should not focus on you, your company, or the features of your product/service. It has to focus on the customer and their needs, wants, and desires. Are we sounding repetitive? Good. Crazy, you say? How will they know who I am and what I do? You'll tell them all that, just not in the headline.

Here are three made-up, bad headlines and the headlines with a marketing makeover.

Example #1

Bad Headline: The Hoover 750 E Has a 40 Horsepower Motor

Better Headline: Get Your Carpets Cleaner, Faster with the Most Powerful Vacuum Ever Made

Example #2

Bad Headline: Johnson Back Clinic: Chiropractic Care Since 1983

Better Headline: Got Back Pain? Get Relief Today at Johnson Back Clinic

Example #3

Bad Headline: SRQ Inc. Offers Honest, Efficient Bookkeeping Services for Small Businesses

Better Headline: Use Your Valuable Time to Make More Money, Not File Your Bills

Sometimes it's just a small shift in language and perspective that can make a big difference. Here's an actual headline from an ad run by a participant in our Marketing Mentor Program and the headline with a marketing makeover.

Before: (Logo) We're Celebrating the 100th Anniversary of the Banana Split

After: Come Celebrate the 100th Anniversary of the Banana Split (moved logo to bottom of ad)

The first headline tells what the company is doing; the second invites the customer to participate in the event.

After reading the first headline the reader thinks, "That's interesting" and moves on. The headline didn't get them personally involved. After reading the second headline, the reader is motivated to continue reading. "Where do I go to celebrate the 100th Anniversary of the Banana Split? When is the celebration?"

Writing a good headline is so important that I suggest you write at least 10 headlines for every marketing piece you create.

Try out different styles, different benefits, different tones, and then pick the best.

There are lots of different types of headlines.

- News headlines.
- Question headlines.
- "How to" headlines.
- Intrigue headlines.
- Guarantee headlines.
- Scare/fear headlines.
- Testimonial headlines.
- Straight benefit headlines.

To inspire you, I share the first list of 12 headlines (and sub-headlines) we wrote when we launched the $17 Solution, "Build a Simple Secret Shopper Program." It took about 15 minutes.

1. Do You Know What Your Employees Are Doing While You're Not Around?

2. Are Your Customers Getting the Service They Deserve— EVERY Time They Shop?
   You Need a Secret Shopper Program to Know For Sure

3. Are Your Employees Stealing Time? Merchandise? Money? Worse?
   It Happens More Often Than You Think

4. What's Going On in *Your* Store When You're Not Around?
   There's Only One Way to Find Out

5. Want to See Your Store Through Your Customer's Eyes?

6. Is Your Staff Doing the Job—Even When You're Not Around?

7. Tired of Employees Who Don't Do What You Want Them to Do?

8. Are They Doing What You Want Them to Do—Even When You're Not There?

9. If Every Major Retailer in America Has a "Secret Shopper" Program, Why Don't *You*?

10. Too Worried about What's Going On in Your Store to Enjoy Your Day Off?
    You Need a Secret Shopper Program!

11. Are Your Employees Giving You Headaches, Nightmares, Ulcers, or *Worse*?

12. Think a Secret Shopper Program Will Cost Too Much or Be a Huge Hassle?
    Think Again.

Which one is your favorite? Which would have motivated *you* to keep reading more about the $17 Solution?

After reviewing, editing, and sleeping on it, we combined a couple, and this is the final headline and subheadline we used:

> What's Going On in Your Store When You're Not Around?
> *If Thinking About It Gives You Headaches,*
> *Nightmares, Ulcers, or WORSE . . .*
> *You Need a Secret Shopper Program!*

When we get work in from our Marketing Mentor Program clients and they haven't used a headline, I'm always afraid my brain may explode, and that makes a big mess in the office, so always have a headline. Thanks.

If you don't get anything else from this copywriting section, please at least learn the three basics.

The Big Three

Here are the three most basic, most important rules of good copywriting for retailers:

1. Make the *big switch* and focus first on your customers, their needs, wants, and desires, not on you, your company, your products or services.
2. Talk about *benefits* first, follow up and support your benefit claims with features.
3. Always have a *headline* for every marketing piece you create, and make sure the headline follows the two rules above.

Used together these three ideas will vastly improve your copywriting skills and make your ads, flyers, brochures, billboards, postcards, websites, in-store signs, letters, posters, anything and *everything* you do, more profitable. That's the bottom line.

Other Concepts to Consider

Of course, the three basic components don't make up all there is to know about copywriting and creating great materials. Not by a long shot! So I briefly mention a few more things to consider.

Conversational Writing

This is a biggie, and it's surprisingly hard for most people to do. When you are writing more than a sentence or two, it's important to keep your writing *conversational*.

Forget all the rules your junior high English teacher taught you. Okay, not all of them. It is important to be grammatically correct and spell things correctly, but you can forget lots of the rules. Like the ones about sentence fragments. Or using slang (words like "long shot" or "biggie"—not offensive or gross language).

This is how we speak when we talk to each other in friendly, conversational situations. Your job as a copywriter is to connect to your prospect on an emotional level, and that usually means as a friend. Someone who can relate to their problems and offer a solution.

One way to get this conversational feel is to pretend you're talking to your best friend over a coffee at your favorite local java joint and telling them about your newest product, special event, latest sale, great offer—take your pick.

Another trick is to actually get a mini-voice recorder and "talk" your ad, letter, or brochure. Then transcribe it, edit for clarity and content, and you'll have something that's probably pretty good.

You definitely don't want your writing to sound as stiff and contrived as a high school term paper. Unfortunately, that's what most people perceive as professional, grown-up writing. It may be, but it's not writing that sells.

Obviously, you can't be very conversational in an ad the size of a business card, but even in a small space you have the choice of using stiff, stilted language or easy, conversational words:

Use instead of *utilize*.

Sign up instead of *register*.

Buy instead of *purchase*.

In longer marketing pieces like brochures or newsletters this conversational style is even more important. Our WhizBang! Tip of the Week is a good example. I'm pretty sure that one of the reasons people like it so much is not only the great *content* of the tips, but the conversational *tone* of the tips. People feel like they know us. The friendly feeling of our Tips creates and cements the personal relationships we have with our readers.

Say One Thing, Sell One Thing

Trying to cram too much information into too small a space is a classic—and potentially catastrophic—marketing mistake. And you see it all the time in everything from yellow pages ads to in-store signs.

Yesterday I went to buy a greeting card for my parents' fiftieth wedding anniversary. On the door into the card shop were no less than *nine* signs in varying sizes, colors, fonts, and designs, with topics ranging from their check cashing policy (don't get me started on that one) to their newest product lines, and the organizations they supported. Good grief! There was so much going on that not a single message made it through the clutter and into my brain.

Same problem happens frequently in newspaper ads. An ad will try to highlight the people's choice award the company won, the service guarantee, the broad selection of merchandise, the weekly special offer, the number of years the company has been in business, *plus* give the address, phone number, and business logo with a tag line in a 3″ × 4″ ad. My head is spinning just thinking about it.

But, hey, we understand why it happens. Those ads aren't cheap and you want to tell as much great stuff about your business as you can to make it worth the money. Problem is, most people just won't retain *anything* if you've overloaded them with information. And then the ad's a real waste of money. Given too many choices or variations, your customer is likely to get confused, befuddled, and frustrated. And then they won't make any buying decision at all.

So whenever you're trying to communicate to your customers in a small space—whether it's the sign on your door, your answering machine message, a newspaper ad, or a direct mail postcard—be very clear about what is most important for them to understand. And say that. Leave out all the extra information and they're more likely to actually receive the one important message you want them to hear.

This means that *before you start writing the first word* of any marketing piece, know what you want the customer *to do*. Come into the store and buy a certain item? Sign up for your email newsletter? Attend a special event you have planned? Click one page further into your website? All of the words you write should be moving your readers toward taking that one action.

Copy Length

This is an interesting topic. Of course, in some formats (postcard, brochure, business card) you're limited on how much you can say and how many words you can use to the size of the space.

But in others—like a letter to hot prospects, for example—there's no preset limit to the length of your copy. Most retailers would guess that you should try to keep it short so people will read it. A whole letter on one page.

Nope. Write as much as it takes to make an airtight, compelling case for your product or service that only a fool would ignore. If it takes you three pages to describe all the benefits of your snowplow service, then by gum write three pages. Don't try to cram them all into one.

In fact, it's been proven time and time again that long copy sells better than short copy. We once bought something from a guy who sent us a *43-page sales letter*! Why, you may be asking yourself, would anyone ever read a 43-page sales letter? Aha . . . Next topic.

Write for Your Target, Not for the Whole World

Of course, most people in the world would *not* have read this guy's 43-page sales letter. Doesn't matter. It matters only if *the people who are predisposed to buy the product or service are interested enough to read the whole letter.* The hot prospects.

Remember that set of concentric circles from the section on affinity marketing? (See Figure 1.7.)

Write directly to your customers and hot prospects, and forget about trying to write something that everyone in the rest of world will read. Write to the people who are already interested in what you are offering.

Create a Compelling Offer

If you're going to bother sending out a marketing piece, make sure it's worth the effort. Create a compelling offer that will motivate someone to shift from reader to customer. To create a compelling offer, do two things. First, make sure you're offering something truly great. If you're not, think about what you can do to boost its value. Even if you *are* offering something great, think about what more

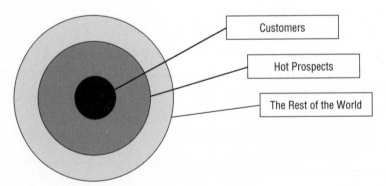

Figure 1.7   The World of Possible Customers.

you can offer to increase the value. Make the offer so good your customers and hot prospects would have to be fools to pass it up.

Here is just one example. A garden center is having a celebrity gardener come for a weekend lecture series and is sending a letter promoting the event.

> *Good offer:* Sign up for the whole series and save $25 on the registration fee.
>
> *Better offer:* Sign up for the whole series and save $25 on the registration fee, attend a special VIP reception and luncheon with the celebrity gardener, and get a free signed copy of the celebrity gardener's latest book.

You can see that without really adding much expense, you've made the offer so interesting that it would be hard for a hard-core, fanatical gardener to resist. Everybody will sign up.

Second, write about it clearly, with vibrant, interesting language. Make the reader *feel* the excitement of meeting the celebrity gardener in person, *desire* the exclusive signed copy of the book, and *understand* the impact the lecture series will have on the quality of their garden. Don't just tell them about the lunch, the book, the lecture.

This is easier to do in longer marketing pieces like letters or flyers, but you can do it in an ad or on a postcard, too. Choose your words carefully to make a compelling offer.

Give a Great Guarantee

Once you've given your prospects every reason in the world to take you up on your compelling offer, go one step further and make sure they have no reason *not* to respond to your message. Take away every roadblock to buying and all their risk. Make it a total no-brainer for them to buy your widget, attend your event, use your new services, or whatever else you're marketing. Help them trust you.

The best way to take away all their risk is to give a great guarantee. We suggest a money-back or better-than-money-back guarantee on pretty much everything. If you believe in the high quality of your goods and services, a great guarantee is an excellent marketing tool.

Remember that guy who sent us the 43-page sales letter? Well, the five-day seminar he was selling wasn't cheap. People had a lot to lose if they went to this event and didn't like it— both time and money. So he offered a *money-back plus $5,000* guarantee if they weren't satisfied at the end of the second day of the workshop. Plus $5,000! No kidding. Talk about taking away all possible risk!

Well, that's what clinched the deal for us. We had absolutely nothing to lose by going and trying it out. Of course, the event was fantastic and not one of the 75 people in attendance even considered leaving at the end of the second day. Not even for $5,000.

I know what you're thinking. "That may have worked for him, but if I give a great guarantee, won't someone take advantage of me." Of course they will! There will always be knuckleheads out there trying to take advantage of others. But if your guarantee attracts many new customers and makes it a no-brainer for lots of people to shop with you, who cares? You'll come out way ahead on the deal. Write about your guarantee in every possible marketing piece.

Issue a Call to Action

One of the copywriting elements most frequently forgotten by business owners is the "call to action." State specifically, directly, and unequivocally what action you want the reader to take. Simply including your phone number, a link, or an order form is *not* enough.

Really. You have to tell them what to do. It's just like selling something in your store. You have to ask the closing question, "Would you like me to ring that up for you?" or "How would you like to pay for that?" Sometimes people need to be prompted to take action.

Issuing a call to action is important in every format, for every marketing piece. In small formats like a yellow pages ad it might look like this:

- Call Now!
- Call Right Now for Your Free Estimate.
- Pick Up the Phone and Call Now.
- Call Today and Have Cleaner Carpets Tomorrow.

In other types of marketing pieces the call might look like this:

- So click on the link below, or cut and paste it into your browser.
- Pick up the phone right now and call 1-800-555-4237 to place your order.
- To register, fill out this order form and fax it to (402) 555-2977, or for faster service, call 1-800-555-4237.

If you've got even more space, try something like this:

- Please pick up the phone right now and call 1-800-432-4243 to reserve your new aqua blue Ultra Widget. Or come on into the store today. As I mentioned, there were only 49 left when I started writing this email and they're flying off the shelf. Get yours before they are all gone.

- As you can probably imagine, we expect this event will be a complete sellout. So call now at 1-800-432-4243, and reserve your seat before they are all gone.

- Just click the Order Now button below to begin your 100 percent secure online checkout. It's fast, easy, and the shipping is *free*!

- Open up your calendar and schedule our "Girls Night Out" event on October 10th. Now forward this email to five of your best girlfriends and make it a party!

We recently got a letter from a local nonprofit group that helps victims of domestic violence with an impassioned plea for help and inviting us to a luncheon benefit for the group. The cause is great, the speaker at the luncheon sounded very interesting, the donation was reasonable. Everything about the letter was great. After reading half the letter we decided to buy tickets to the luncheon.

But they didn't tell us what to do! No phone number (except the one on the letterhead), no registration form, no option to pay by credit card, no contact name of a person to whom we could ask questions, no website address, not even an address where we should send the check.

We did contribute, but by the time we figured out where to send the check and got the tickets back in the mail, the luncheon had passed. And we began to wonder about the efficient use of our funds.

Don't make your customers guess what they are supposed to do or make them hunt for your address, phone number, or fax. Tell them exactly what you want them to do and make it as easy as possible for them to do it.

Add a P.S.

It's a psychological thing. Human beings are just plain attracted to that P.S. at the end of a letter.

It's supposed to be an afterthought, something you forgot to mention in the body of your letter and then later felt was important enough to add. And that's intriguing. What could be so important that you had to add it later—after the letter was completed? Of course, rationally we all know that in today's age of computerized word processing you could easily go back in and add anything you thought you had missed, but emotionally the mystique of the P.S. remains.

In fact, lots of really hot copywriters believe that the P.S. is an extremely important element of writing in your marketing piece—*second only to your headline*. I'm not sure if that's true, but I do know that you'll get a better response with a P.S. than without one.

Include a P.S. with every marketing piece that reads like a letter. Of course, a P.S. won't necessarily work with a display ad or a brochure but there are lots of times when you can use the P.S. to your advantage.

Many readers will actually flip to the P.S. and read it before they begin reading the body of the letter so it's kind of like a second headline. Your job with the P.S. is to make them interested enough in what you're saying to get them to start reading. It's also the last thing people will read, so restate the strongest part of your message. It may be the product benefit, your guarantee, the amazing offer, or the tip that positions you as an expert. Reiterate your call to action and remind the reader what you want them to do.

Here are some examples:

- P.S. As you know, this is a limited edition print, with only 200 being offered. Please reserve yours before they are all gone. Call 1-800-555-4243 now, as there is no time to waste.

- P.S. A full night's sleep can be yours—*drug free*—with the *new* patented sleep pillow. Order by March 1 and I'll throw in a free copy of my special report "How to Dream Away the Pounds While You Sleep."

- P.S. If you want to own this ball, you'd better move faster than Carlos Delgado's bat because baseball fans all over the country will be clamoring after this piece of World Series history. Call me right away at 800-555-1212.

- P.S. With WhizBang! Websites you get a comprehensive email marketing system, a great-looking website you can change and update yourself, and most importantly essential how-to information from e-marketing expert Bob Negen. Sign up today at www.whizbangwebsites.com.

Because your P.S. is so important, write several in different styles. Later you can edit, revise, and then pick your favorite.

Hot Tip!

If you want to delve deeper into the subject of copywriting, check out the additional resources we have listed on the Retailer Resource page of our website: www.whizbangtraining.com.

We've separated the wheat from the chaff and listed our favorite ebooks, online courses, and boot camps—the ones that will actually be helpful for retailers.

So Much More   There's much more to great copywriting, but if you will really focus on the three basic rules for good copywriting we covered earlier in this section, your marketing materials will be head and shoulders above the crowd.

The Ten Commandments of Copywriting for Retailers

1. Always Have a Headline.

2. Don't Use Your Business Name or Logo as Your Headline.

3. Write From Your Customer's Point of View.

4. Use More Benefits, Less Features.

5. Understand Precisely Why You Are Writing Your Ad.

6 Write with Emotion.

7. Keep Your Language Conversational.

8. Create a Compelling Offer.

9. Give a Great Guarantee.

10. Issue a Call to Action.

P.S. Add a strong P.S. It's the second thing people read after the headline.

If you *use all* 10 of the Ten Commandments of Copywriting for Retailers, you'll be in a class all your own. Go ahead and rip out the preceding page and post it near the computer you use most when you are writing your marketing materials. Or make a photocopy of it. Or go to our website and download the free PDF poster from our Retailer Resources page. Use these techniques in each and every piece of writing you do.

Turn a First-Time Buyer into a Regular Customer

Two Key Concepts for Turning a First-Time Buyer into a Regular Customer

These marketing ideas are the foundation for any truly successful independent retailer. Once you've attracted a new customer by using the tactics in the previous section and they have come into your store or made a visit to your website, then the real work begins. And the real fun. And the biggest profits.

Key Concept #1: Lifetime Value of a Customer

Shortsighted businesspeople like to make the fastest possible dollar: in-and-out. Smart businesspeople spend time with their customers and get to know them. They find out what they like and dislike, and they learn how their customers feel.

Customers are not "one-shot wonders." They are the lifeblood of your business. A good customer will use your services many times over the course of many years and will refer their friends, family, and business associates to you.

Simply put, the "lifetime value" of your customer is the *total dollar amount they will spend with you before they take their business somewhere else, move away, or die.* Smart businesspeople do everything they can to nurture relationships and increase the lifetime value of their customers.

You may not have the sort of detailed records you need to determine the actual average lifetime value of your customers. Most businesspeople don't, but that shouldn't stop you from building long-term, even lifelong relationships with your new customers and perhaps starting to keep track of that information.

Eventually you'll be able to figure out a dollar amount value that an average customer spends on your services over a period of years. Some customers may be worth only $50 to your business over their lifetime, but some may be worth $5,000. It's the average that's important.

Key Concept #2: The Big Switch

We know of only one surefire, never-fail, superprofitable strategy for battling the big boys.

Always put your customers' wants, needs, and desires first.

I call it The Big Switch. The secret to success is to fall out of love with your products, services, or store, and fall in love with your customers. They are the absolute, number one most important part of your business. Without your customers there would be no need for your store, your products, or your services.

When you make The Big Switch, all your business decisions suddenly revolve around what's best for your customers, not what's most convenient for you.

- Your store hours will fit your customers' schedule, not yours.
- Your product assortment will reflect what your customer likes, not what you like.
- Your store policies will be written with your customers' best interests in mind.
- Your return policies will be generous, not restrictive.
- Your staff will be thoroughly trained so your customers get the same great service from everyone in your store that they get from you.
- Your store layout will be designed from your customers' point of view.

The list goes on and on, but it all starts with making The Big Switch and looking at everything you do through the eyes of your customers. When you make The Big Switch, you stop looking at your customer as a single transaction, someone standing at your register with a credit card in their hand, and start looking at your customer as a person with whom you have a deep and meaningful long-term relationship.

It is this ability to create and nurture your customer relationships that is your biggest competitive advantage. No matter how they may try, the big boys can't beat you at this game. While they have the size advantage when it comes to price and selection, you have the distinct size advantage when it comes to loving your customer.

> *You have a face and a personality*: all they have is a brand.
>
> *You can know your customers personally*: they can only know a set of statistics.

When you love your customers, the money will follow. By putting your customer's needs, wants, and desires first, you will dramatically increase the lifetime value of that customer—the total amount that person will spend with you over their life as your customer.

When you love your customers and nurture your relationship properly, they will shop with you more often, spend more each time they shop, stay with your company more years, and send their family, friends, and colleagues to your store.

Let me share my personal "Aha!" experience with you—the moment when this concept was permanently embedded in my brain. I was working on the sales floor of the Mackinaw Kite Co. helping a youngish grandmother pick out some gifts for her five grandchildren. Always one to do a little market research when the opportunity presented itself, I asked her how often she would be shopping for gifts for her grandchildren. I thought I was asking about the number of times a year she shopped, or on which holidays she shopped for gifts, but her answer stopped me dead in my tracks. "*Forever.*"

Of course! She would indeed be shopping for gifts for her grandkids forever. Now, my eyes must have glazed over as my mental calculator started whirring. She had five grandchildren, and there were at least three gift purchases a year that I could count on (birthdays, Christmas, and Easter), and our average sale was about $50—that's $750 a year. And she would probably be buying gifts for at least another 15 years.

In an instant, this woman was worth nearly $12,000 to me, not just the $29.99 she was plunking down at the moment.

I knew then that I had to do everything in my power to love this customer and keep her coming to my store for as long as she was buying gifts for her grandchildren. My goal? A customer for life.

My challenge to you is to make the Big Switch. Fall out of love with your product, service, or store and fall in love with your customers. Make it your goal to create customers for life. We're all in business to make money, and the surest way to make money is to love your customers.

Three Low-Tech Tactics for Turning a First-Time Buyer into a Regular Customer

This section of the book focuses on a very short window of time in the life span of your customer. We key in on the very first time a prospect becomes a customer. It's a critical time in your relationship with your customer and holds the key to your future success with that particular person. The beginning.

I've talked about beginning a relationship with a customer in many different ways, but the best way I've found to get my point across is to talk about a love relationship. We've all had them and can all relate to the process. Beginning, middle, and hopefully no end.

So as we talk about these low-tech tactics, Bob tells you a love story. Now this story could be a boy meets boy story, or a girl meets girl story, but since it is *our* story, it's a "Boy Meets Girl" story. The story of how we met.

Turn Them into A Regular Customer Tactic #1: *Give a Great First Experience in Your Store*

Our relationship began and grew the same way that nearly every other relationship does and the same way your relationship to the customers you want to have personal, lasting relationships with should begin.

You meet. Seems self-evident, but it's true that before you can really have a relationship with someone, you have to meet them. Before you meet, you may admire them, desire them, or be interested in them, but you don't have a relationship with them.

I met Susan in a bar. Not as cheesy as it sounds when you consider that I was introduced to her by a friend. An old girlfriend to be precise. Hey, word-of-mouth advertising works!

Anyway, I learned her name, she learned mine. We chatted. Laughed. Had an interesting conversation. We learned a little bit about each other. Found out we like the same kind of music and had both vacationed in Mexico. She flirted with me; I flirted back.

In your business you "meet" your customers when you make that first solid contact—usually a sale. You can't count someone walking by and window shopping as a "meet." You usually can't count a browser as a "meet." That's like locking eyes with someone across a crowded room but never speaking to them. The interest is there, but you haven't really met them.

For a few of you with very expensive products or a long sales process the meet probably takes place well before you make a sale. But the concept applies: Unless you have had a significant interaction, you haven't really met your customer.

Back to me and Susan that very first night in the bar. What do you think would have happened if the conversation had lagged, we had nothing in common, or my breath had been stinky? Right—not much.

It was not only the fact that we met each other that night which led to our eventual relationship, it was the quality of the meeting. We liked each other! I liked her and so I did my best to make sure she liked me. I was charming, witty, and suave. Well, that's the way I remember it anyway.

The same thing holds true when you meet your customer for

the first time. This is the moment when the rubber meets the road. All of your efforts at attracting new customers will be in vain if, at your first meeting, your prospect doesn't like your store.

If someone buys something from you but has a ho-hum or downright bad experience in your store, you have a one-time buyer—but not a regular customer. And getting that customer to come back and buy from you again, and again, and again is where the big money is. You have to give them a *great* in-store experience so they'll be interested in continuing their relationship with you.

Interestingly enough, your customer is probably judging their experience in your store in the same way they would judge a person at the beginning of a love relationship. Am I physically attracted? Do we have something in common? Are they nice to me? Is there any spark? If they answer *yes* to these questions about your store, there's no doubt that you're on the way to turning that first-time buyer into a regular customer.

We could probably write a whole book just on delivering a great in-store experience. In this section we just highlight a few of the basic things you must do to market your business while the customer is actually on your selling floor.

Sparkling Clean   This is the very foundation of a great customer experience in your store. But it's amazing how many stores you go into that are dirty, dusty, and dingy. The message it sends to your customer is that you don't care enough about them to make the effort. A dirty store also sends a message about the quality of your products and services.

Your store windows and doors should be cleaned at least once a day, the floors vacuumed daily, and all fixtures, shelves, and racks dusted regularly. Make sure all the light bulbs are working. Here's a pet peeve of ours: Make sure all the dead flies and dust bunnies are sucked up out of the corners of your display windows. Yuck!

It's equally important that the outside of your store is clean and well cared for. Sweep the sidewalks (or shovel if there's snow) every morning. Pay special attention to the entryway, and make sure there are no clinging bugs, webs, sprouting weeds, cigarette butts, blowing trash, or other unsightly stuff. The outside of your store is the first glimpse your new customer will have of you, and they are forming opinions before they even get out of their car.

Hot Tip!

Finding inexpensive but effective ways to improve your store design isn't always easy. We've found a truly great resource for you that will help give you wonderful ideas to revitalize your storefront.

Check it out on the Retailer Resources page of our website: www.whizbangtraining.com.

Updated and Fresh Store Design   If your store looks like it belongs in the 1970s, the carpet was last replaced two decades ago, and you can't remember the last time you painted, it's time for an update.

Your store design, your fixtures, and the quality, style, and quantity of your lighting are important cues to your customer about what kind of place you're running. And how much you care about their business.

We recently read an article about a top East Coast drugstore that lowered all of its fixtures to five feet so the average woman— who is five feet four inches tall—can easily see around the store and reach all the items. They painted the walls warm, vibrant colors. And their sales are skyrocketing! They've changed their store design to be more attractive to their customers, and the customers are responding.

If your date shows up in a leisure suit and white loafers it gives one kind of first impression, old jeans and a T-shirt give you another, and stylish new clothes give another. What does your store design and layout say about you?

A Well Stocked Store   Your merchandise assortment is a critical component in creating a great first impression. In fact, along with staff management and marketing we think that inventory management is one of the three keystones in creating a truly successful retail store.

But being well stocked doesn't just mean having a whole bunch of stuff in your store. It means having the *right amount* of the *right stuff* at the *right time*. It means never running out of best sellers. It means relentlessly pursuing new items that your customers will love and dumping old styles that they don't like. It means having the right mix of basics, accessories, trend, and image merchandise.

It's easy to say, but trickier to do. That's why so few retail stores really have a grip on their merchandise assortment and inventory control. It's hard! And it's not something you're born knowing how to do. If you feel like this is an area you're doing by the seat of your pants—buying merchandise without any sort of strategic plan—go learn something about it. Susan learned how to do this when she worked at big department stores and in turn Bob learned it from her at the Mackinaw Kite Co., and now our clients are learning from her through our Inventory Mastery Program. Be a learner.

The bottom line is that your customers come to your store to buy something. To fill a need or satisfy a desire. You must offer the merchandise they want and need to deliver a great in-store experience.

Well Displayed Merchandise   You can carry great merchandise, but if it's not well displayed your customers won't know it. To give a great in-store experience, make your goods appealing, easy to find, and grouped together in a logical fashion.

While it helps to have a natural flair for display, you don't really have to be artistic or creative to have well displayed merchandise. One important technique to remember is to keep all of your fixtures consistent. Using a whole bunch of different vendor fixtures is a sure path to bad display—even if those fixtures *were* free. Keep your displays simple and uncluttered so that the merchandise is easy to see. Too much visual confusion will cause shoppers to "shut down" and look for a calmer space—outside your store maybe?

Good Signage   Good signs are an easy way to create a good in-store experience. Some signs help your customers navigate around your store and give them information they want to know. These signs are usually large enough to read from far away and let people know where they can find certain types of merchandise: Games, Construction Toys, Dolls, Baby Toys, Trains. Sometimes signs point out service areas: Check Out, Restroom, Fitting Rooms.

Some signs give information about a specific piece of merchandise. Merchandise signs act as salespeople to customers who are too shy to ask questions. They are your stand-in during the information gathering part of the buying process. Signs make your merchandise more attractive to customers by highlighting interesting features, hidden benefits, or outstanding value. Signs can help turn browsers into buyers.

Unfortunately, making signs is one of those tasks that frequently gets brushed aside. If you have a computer and printer you can make great signs. Keep your font style, size, and color consistent for all your merchandise signs. Make sure they are easy to read and not overly complicated. *Always* have a benefit headline for every merchandise sign. Follow up with some additional information and possibly the price. Here's an example.

Your Best Bet for Ground Cover in Shady Spots
Sweet Woodruff is a shade gardener's delight.
Fast-growing and quick to establish, with beautiful white spring
flowers and attractive foliage through to snow,
this treasure is seldom bothered by pest or disease.
$9.99 for a small flat

Put your signs in sturdy good-looking sign holders. Clear Plexi-glas always works well and they are very easy to find. If you have a very fashion oriented store or a very traditional store, you could use other styles of frames to hold your signs. But be consistent with your sign holders to give a clean, uncluttered look to the store. And for goodness sake, don't tape the signs up! You're not running a lemonade stand.

An Amazing Staff   Your staff is frequently the make or break part of your customers' first experience in your store. If they get great service or topnotch product information, they will really like your store. If they get ignored, or get uninformed, uninspired help, they won't be back.

One of the toughest parts of any retailer's job is to develop a staff that gives each and every customer the service they deserve, each and every time. It's a six-step process:

1. Find 'Em.
2. Interview 'Em.
3. Hire 'Em.
4. Train 'Em.
5. Coach 'Em.
6. And if they don't work out—Fire 'Em.

Understanding and perfecting this process is a keystone for re-tail success. These folks are your representatives in the store and are standing face-to-face with your customers every day. Without great employees you can't have great long-lasting relationships with your customers. And you can't give a great in-store experience.

If you have a staff full of highly trained, superstar employees, congratulations! If you need some help in this area, check out our website: We have lots of great reports, kits, articles, and tips to help you build a WhizBang! Staff.

Great Selling   Some people don't like to "sell" to their customers. They just like to let them browse around and buy if they want to. Mistake! Most customers want help when they are in your store—even if they say, "Just looking."

Selling is not a dirty word. Great selling is not pushy, rude, or an invasion of the customer's privacy. Great selling is great cus-tomer service.

If your first-time customer comes in and is greeted promptly with genuine openness, has a good connection with their salesper-son, and leaves with everything they want and need to make their purchase a success—*that* is a great in-store experience and that's what you get with great selling.

Customer-Friendly Policies   Everything from your store hours to your return policy should be customer-friendly, customer-focused, and designed to make your customer smile. Strive to eliminate all barriers to buying.

Now I know that some of you are worried that people will take advantage of your generous policies. It's true. A few people might. But would you give away a little bit to gain a whole lot? I hope your answer is yes.

Offering longer, customer-convenient store hours is such a sticking point for so many retail store owners and *we just don't get it.*

Ten in the morning until five in the evening, shortened Saturday hours and closed on Sundays might have been just fine in the 1970s, but it's a whole new world out there. These kinds of hours just don't cut it anymore. Keep these hours today and your primary customers will be the unemployed.

People can shop 24 hours a day, 7 days a week at the local superstore, on the Internet, and with catalog merchants. Yet quite often they have to work very hard to shop with the independent merchants and other small businesses in their own neighborhoods.

One of the most important things you can do is to make it as easy as humanly possible for your customers to shop with you. And you cannot sell through a closed door. Your hours should be tailored to the schedule of your customers, not to your schedule. This means staying open *all day* on Saturday, staying open late on at least some weekdays, and opening on Sundays.

Quite often this means hiring and training new people. Many store owners are hesitant to take on the extra cost and responsibilities of longer hours. In this case it pays.

Seimens Research did a survey and found that during the two-hour segment on Saturday between 12:00 and 2:00 P.M. 11 percent of Americans were shopping. From 2:00 to 4:00 P.M. on Saturday was the next-busiest shopping segment, followed by 12:00 to 2:00 on Sunday, then 2:00 to 4:00 on Sunday. So if you're not open on Saturday afternoon and on Sunday, you're missing the four busiest shopping times in the United States.

If you want to stay in business in today's incredibly competitive retail environment, put the needs, wants, and desires of your customers first. This means longer hours, hours that fit the schedules of today's superbusy consumer.

The Wow! Factor   Little things make the biggest difference. In the little extra touches we can do better than the big boys, which add up to an overall impression of "Wow!"

"Wow! That was fun."

"Wow! That was interesting."

"Wow! That was easy."

"Wow! That was more than I expected."

"Wow! That was a special touch."

What can you do in your store to give your customers a Wow! experience? Here are just a few examples to get you thinking.

- At the Mackinaw Kite Co. we tied a snap swivel onto every spool of kite line we sold and gave the customer a "free lesson in kite line retrieval." It made the kite flying experience much better and the in-store experience more fun.

- One of our garden center clients gives away a special package of sunflower seeds, soil, and a small pot to every child who comes in with their parent. An exciting gift that the kids look forward to year after year.

- An ice cream store puts a piece of candy corn upside down in the end of every cone—to prevent the dreaded bottom drips as the ice cream slowly melts.

- Our local gourmet store has been around for 94 years, and they still take the price tag off your wine bottle before it goes into your bag. Who wants to remember how much you paid for that bottle when it's time to pop the cork?

- An upscale gift store not only gift wraps your purchase for you, but has an entire alphabet of rubber stamps and will put the re- cipient's monogram on the gift for you. It makes your gift extra special.

You can see that not one of these ideas costs very much, takes very much time, or is hard to do. They are all simple ideas that come from thinking about the customer's experience and how it could be enhanced.

All of these elements, from a sparkling clean store to that little extra Wow! make your customer's experience special and turn that first-time buyer into a regular, lifelong customer.

Turn Them into a Regular Customer Tactic #2: Ask For Their Contact Information

Back once again to the courtship of Bob and Susan. As it happens, I was planning a dinner party for the day after I met Susan. Since we were having a nice conversation there in the bar, I asked her if she'd like to come.

The party was fun: She liked my friends, they liked her, and I nailed the Beef Zinfandel I had prepared for dinner. By the end of the evening I knew I wanted to see her again, so I asked for permission to continue the relationship *by asking for her phone number.* Without any way to get in touch with her, there would be no way for me to pursue the relationship. Not a great start to a close and lasting relationship. So if I wanted to see her again, I had to ask for her number.

By giving me her phone number she was letting me know that it was okay for me to call and keep things moving forward. *Permission.* Of course, I could have just waited around and *hoped* that we'd run into each other again some evening, but by now you know how we feel about "hope marketing."

You've probably guessed where this is heading as it relates to your business. Get the contact information for your customers if you want to develop a close, personal, profitable relationship with them. By giving you this information they are giving you permission to continue developing your relationship with them. They are giving you permission to contact them.

We recommend that you ask for the street address and email address of every single customer at the point of sale.

Make it your store standard that every employee asks every customer, every time. The consistency is the trick. Employees don't just ask when they feel like it, when the customer is nice, or when they've made a big sale. They ask every customer, every time.

You can do a couple of things to make it easier for the employee to ask, and more likely that the customer will give you the information. First, come up with some reasons for the customer to give you their information—some benefits to being on your mailing list. What will they get from you? Special reports? Special offers? Advance notice of sales? If you include mention of your privacy policy, this will also make customers feel more comfortable giving you their personal information.

One of the best angles is to invite the customer to join your Preferred Customer Club. If they join the club they fill out the registration form, which automatically includes their name, address, and email address. You don't really even have to ask for it. For lots more on the Preferred Customer Club tactic, check the next section of the book, Step 3: Get Your Customers to Shop More Often.

Explain to your staff exactly why it's in the customer's best interest to sign up for the mailing list or Preferred Customer Club and give them specific language to use when telling the customer about it. One of the most common reasons employees don't ask every customer for their information is that they are uncomfortable asking the question. They don't know what to say. If you give them the words, it will be easier for them and you're more likely to get more names in the list. To make them even more comfortable asking for addresses, have them do role plays with each other and also coach them on their real efforts asking customers at the cash register.

Sometimes employees will stop asking during busy times—like Saturdays, holidays, or other busy times. Sometimes the store owner tells them to stop asking! We know this might seem like a good idea to move people through the checkout process faster, but think again.

You need each and every one of those names so you can generate business in the slower times. The better solution is to come up with ways to solve the problem of long lines at the cash register, not stop asking for names. Instead of adding the names directly into the computer, maybe you have them fill out a form while they're waiting in line. The Preferred Customer Club works very well in this situation. Maybe you should add additional POS computers during these busy times of the year. Or maybe you can have one employee ringing and one getting names and addresses.

Your customer list is so valuable and so important that you should do whatever it takes to capture those names—especially during the busy times of the year. Remember: Without that contact information you'll have no choice but to sit around and *hope* that your one-time customer comes back to shop with you again.

Turn Them into a Regular Customer Tactic #3: Follow Up Immediately

How many of you think it would have gone well if I had invited Susan to my dinner party, asked for her phone number, and then called her back, say, three months later? Yeah. That's what she says, too.

Instead, I called her the next day and asked her to the movies—

or maybe it was out for coffee. The point is I called her right away. And that's what you need to do, too. When someone is kind enough to give you their personal contact information it's just polite to contact them right away and say thanks. Let them know you care about the fledgling relationship. In fact, it may be counterproductive to ask for someone's contact information and then never send them anything. Or send them something six months later.

Follow Up Immediately   Set up a system for sending a handwritten follow-up card for every new person who joins your mailing list. Handwritten cards or notes have the advantage of being very personal, and remember we are trying to build relationships here, but cards or notes take more time and therefore are more likely to get put off. Preprinted materials are somewhat easier but are definitely less personal. Use these only if you absolutely have to.

Now those of you who have high volume businesses are probably thinking I'm *nuts*. That you can never do it. But if your personal relationships are your biggest advantage over the corporate competition, can you afford not to?

They Did It ...

A Michigan florist sends a handwritten note to every new customer. A few days after receiving one of these notes one of these new customers came back and insisted she see the person who wrote her the note.

This customer did not buy anything on this particular trip to the store; she just wanted to thank the employee for the thoughtful gesture.

The florist commented, "She didn't buy anything that day, but judging from her enthusiasm for the card, it's safe to say she'll never buy flowers anywhere else."

... You Can, Too!

Several things we have found make this process go much more smoothly and most importantly, keep the system going. First, put one person on your staff in charge of the program. Maybe that person is you, maybe a manager, an assistant manager, or a team leader. Whoever it is should have good organizational skills and great follow-through. Having one person in charge of the program will ensure consistency and accuracy.

Set a standard for what the cards should look like and make sure the materials needed to write the cards are easily available. Always use the same kind of note card or letterhead, color of ink (you think this direction is crazy until the first time an employee writes a card in green ink), envelope, and stamp. Gather all the materials in one place—maybe a folder or a box—and make sure it stays full. Not having materials to write the notes is a stumbling block that can easily derail your thank-you note program.

Decide who is going to write the notes. Is it you? Someone else assigned the job? The salesperson who helped the customer? The best case scenario is that the salesperson who helped the customer, rang them up, and signed them up for the mailing list immediately writes the note. This way they can include a personalized touch to the message based on their interaction with the customer. "Hope your new Aqua Blue Ultra Widget looks great with the paint color in your living room." Of course this best case scenario won't always happen, so get a backup plan in place.

We definitely recommend that you come up with a template message and set parameters for message writing. Determine an appropriate greeting, body text, and closing. Don't assume your employees will automatically write the kind of note you want sent from your store.

We find that even using a template note, it is always a good idea to have the program manager quickly read through the notes before they are sent. We once had a great employee who got tired of writing the standard greeting "Dear Name," and we caught him sending a thank-you that started "O Ye of Brighton!" He just thought it might be fun to spice things up. We reminded him that the customer hadn't received hundreds of notes that said the same thing—even though he had written that many.

Here's our sample thank-you note.

Dear <Customer Name>,

Thank you so much for coming in to see us at <Your Store Name>.
<Insert a personalized sentence here like: "I hope your husband loves the Double Mocha Chip Ice Cream Cake you ordered for this birthday.">
We appreciate your business and look forward to seeing you again soon.

Warm regards,

Your Name

You can see that the note doesn't have to be long, or fancy, or time consuming. It just has to be a sincere thank-you and it has to get done. The most important thing is to let the customer know you recognize that they were in your store and that you care about it.

Finally, decide when you are going to send them. Are you going to write and send the cards at the end of every shift? Every day? Once a week? Make sure they get written and get sent.

Two High-Tech Tactics for Turning a First-Time Buyer into a Regular Customer

These two tactics are the high-tech versions of the preceding tactics. The high-tech tactics have the advantage of being automatic, which makes them very easy for you.

Turn Them into a Regular Customer Tactic #4: Have a Newsletter Sign-Up on Your Website

In this high-tech version of Ask For Their Contact Information, you gather customer contact information—specifically names and email addresses—by including a sign-up box on every page of your website. Every time they meet you on the Web, ask them for permission to continue the relationship.

Using a sign-up box, have them sign up to get your e-newsletter, join your Preferred Customer Club, or register for your group. Figure 2.1 shows four sample sign-up boxes: two from our WhizBang! Tip of the Week, one from a garden center newsletter, and one from a home furnishings store that specializes in merchandise from Bali.

In the sign-up box give some very short information about what they are signing up for. On one of your website pages *fully* explain the benefits of receiving the newsletter, highlight your privacy policy, and issue a strong invitation (also known as the call to action) to sign up. Link to this from your home page.

You may want to give a sample newsletter or have an archive of your most recent emails so that readers can see for themselves what sort of messages you'll be sending. They want to make sure you won't be sending boring, spam-ey emails. *Note:* You'll learn lots more on how to use email marketing and email lists in the section of the book on getting customers to shop with you more often.

Exactly what happens when someone signs up via the box on your website may vary depending on the programming of your site, but usually the name and email address are added directly to the customer list for your email server. This means that the next time you send your email newsletter, they are automatically on the list to receive the message.

Figure 2.1   **Sample Sign-Up Boxes.**

With WhizBang! Websites, the website with sign-up box and the email marketing functions are completely integrated so this happens seamlessly. And with our standalone WhizBang! Email (no website attached) you can cut and paste provided HTML code for a sign-up box onto your existing website. When someone signs up they are automatically added to your WhizBang! Email list.

Having a sign-up box on every page of your website tells your customers, "Hey, we want to know you—and we want to give you something valuable or beneficial in return." Just like the guy asking the girl for her phone number, it expresses interest in continuing the relationship. Your job is to make sure your website is interesting enough that the visitor will want to continue having a relationship with *you*.

Turn Them into a Regular Customer Tactic #5: Create Automatic Welcome Emails

This is the high-tech version of Follow Up Immediately. When someone signs up for your newsletter by entering their name and email in the box on your website, send them a "Welcome" email.

It is especially important in cyberspace to let people know that you've received their information and to thank them for agreeing to share it with you. If they click the Submit button and nothing happens, they are going to feel like the woman who gives out her phone number but never gets a call. They don't even have the memory of a nice human being taking their information, smiling, and saying Thank-you.

Many email list servers will automatically send out a confirmation email to the person who has submitted their email to let them know their sign-up was successful. This is a good start. *If at all possible customize and personalize your welcome email—not just use the default message created by the programmer.*

You are trying to begin and develop personal relationships and a message that reads "Sign up confirmed. You are subscribed to www.yourdomainname.com" isn't going to make your new customer feel all warm and fuzzy! Just because your email is getting sent automatically doesn't mean it has to sound automated.

You need to send a welcome email that confirms that their decision to sign up for your newsletter was a good one, that gives them something of value, and that has a warm, personal feeling to it, even though it *is* getting sent by a machine.

See Figure 2.2 for an example of the welcome email we

Welcome to the "WhizBang! Tip of the Week"

Thank you for letting us share our favorite shortcuts to success.

We promise your tips will be short, practical, profitable, and fun. They're kind of like a good cup of coffee—a midweek professional pick-me-up.

Want to check out our past WhizBang! Tips? Just go to the TIPS section of our website, www.whizbangtraining.com/sb. You'll also find lots of free reports and articles on our site. Yours to enjoy!

Here is your first tip—it's one of our past tips that was a big hit with all of the Tip of the Weekers. We hope you'll enjoy it, too. From now on you'll be on the regular Tip of the Week schedule along with everyone else.

TIP********TIP********TIP********TIP********TIP*******TIP*******TIP

Ten Telephone Tips

You and your staff *can* give the very best customer service on the phone. Like so many other things in life, it's the little details that make the biggest difference.

- Focus on the phone call you are about to take. Make a conscious mental shift from your last customer, task, or conversation. Don't answer the phone while you are still talking to someone else.

- Take a deep breath, exhale, and *smile* before you answer the phone. Your smile will come through in your voice even though your caller can't see you.

- Put a mirror by the phone if possible to remind yourself to smile and sit or stand straight.

- Always give your business name and your name when you answer. The caller wants to know they have reached the right place and whom they are talking to.

- Speak slowly and articulate your words—especially your greeting. Make sure it doesn't sound like, "WhizBangTrainingthisissusan."

Figure 2.2   Welcome Email for WhizBang! Tip of the Week.

- Use proper English and avoid slang. You're not addressing your buddies, but your business contacts.

- Be sure to say, "Thank you" at the end of every call. There's always a reason to thank a customer for making the effort to contact your company.

- The "good-bye" is as important as the "hello." Make sure your caller has finished with everything they want to say before you hang up. Wait for them to say good-bye and hang up before you replace the receiver.

- If you are leaving a message on a customer's (or vendor's, or anyone's) answering machine, it's especially important that you say your name and the company name clearly. You may even want to spell it if there is any question.

- When leaving an answering machine message, leave your return phone number even if you think they already have it. Make sure you say the number distinctly and *slowly*. Remember, they are writing this number down and it is annoying to have to rewind the message several times to get it. Another good trick is to repeat your name, company name, and telephone number at the very end of your message.

TIP********TIP********TIP********TIP********TIP*******TIP*******TIP

We'd love to hear your favorite telephone success stories—or your telephone nightmare stories! Send them to tips@whizbangtraining.com, and we'll pass along your great ideas.

Wishing you great sales and lots of fun,

Bob and Susan Negen
WhizBang! Training
Phone: 616-842-4237
Fax: 616-842-2977
Email: tips@whizbangtraining.com
212 South Harbor Dr. #301
Grand Haven, MI 49417

Figure 2.2 *(Continued)*

automatically send out when someone signs up for our WhizBang! Tip of the Week.

With this email we are trying to start our new relationship off on the right foot. It's coming directly from us; it's not a generic, "no person actually wrote this" sounding message. It's friendly, informative, and gives our names and contact information.

A Welcome Campaign   If your email server allows you to create email campaigns—a predetermined set of emails sent at specific intervals—it can be very effective to send a series of emails welcoming your new customer and informing them about you, your store, your newsletter, and making some great offers.

This is an especially good idea if you don't send frequent newsletters, say only once a month or once a quarter. Cement your relationship with the customer before you disappear from their radar.

Here's a scenario for a four-email welcome campaign for an outdoor outfitters store:

Day of sign-up: Welcome and sample of past newsletter.

Four days after sign-up: A virtual store tour (pictures in the email), information about the products carried, and some funny/interesting stories about the store owner and staff. Invitation to visit the store with a $10 gift certificate.

Twelve days after signup: A schedule of events for the upcoming year along with pictures from last year's events.

Twenty-four days after sign-up: A list of the best canoeing and kayaking spots within a 25-mile radius (summer) or the best hiking and cross country ski trails (winter). Include a sales pitch for related products.

You can see how a series of emails like this would really make a new customer feel great about this store. And drive sales.

The beautiful thing about email campaigns—also sometimes called autoresponders—is that you just have to write the emails and set up the campaigns *once*. Then when someone signs up for your list, the email series automatically starts sending to their address, each email on the particular day you have set. You don't have to *do* anything!

This is one of the great features we built into WhizBang! Email. You can send Welcome Campaigns as well as many other different kinds of email campaigns. Cheap, quick, and easy.

You can see that while a low-tech tactic of sending handwritten notes to everyone who signs up in your store is superpersonal but time consuming, this high-tech tactic is supereasy but not quite as personal. You won't be able to mention a specific conversation you've shared or ask how they like the product they just purchased using an automatic welcome letter. But there is merit to both, and we recommend that you use a blend of both the low-tech and the high-tech tactics.

Get Your Customers to Shop More Often

Now we are at the most profitable and fun part of the life cycle of your customer. You've attracted a prospect to your business, they have made a first purchase, and you've captured their contact information. They are now a *real* customer.

At this point deepen and strengthen your relationship with that customer. Just as in the "Boy Meets Girl" story this is the point in the relationship when you hang out together, get to know each other better, and fall in love.

The object, then, of marketing to current customers is to get them to come into your store consistently and frequently—to spend time with you. You are working to build that "I'd never shop anywhere else" loyalty—to fall in love.

The good news is that marketing to your existing customers is easier and cheaper than trying to attract new customers. Selling your existing customers more stuff, more often is the most important and most profitable way to build your business.

If you could take every single existing customer you have and get them to shop with you just *one extra time this year*, how much would that mean for you in extra sales? Well, if you have a customer base of 500 people and an average sale of $50, it's an extra $25,000 a year. Not bad!

Note to New Businesses: Some of you may have a brand new business with no, or very few, current customers. You may be thinking that this section isn't important for you, that all you need to work on is getting new customers. Well, while you may need to put more emphasis on getting lots of new customers than a well-established business, you must still *start* by developing tactics to use with existing customers, because the moment you get that very first customer you *must* do everything you can to maximize their potential benefit to your company. And the same thing with the second, third, and so on.

If you don't have the tactics, tools, and systems in place to market to existing customers, you'll be losing valuable time and momentum. In fact, by having a strategic plan for marketing to existing customers in place before you actually have any customers, you'll be miles ahead of most of your competition. And your success will come more quickly and more easily than you ever thought possible.

Two Key Concepts to Get Your Customers to Shop More Often

These are the key marketing concepts to keep in mind as you think about the tactics that follow. In particular, pay very close attention to "The Secret Strategy" presented in key concept #2—it really is the magic formula for creating super loyal customers who will never shop anywhere else.

Key Concept #1: It's Your Responsibility to Be Remembered, Not Your Customer's Responsibility to Remember You

Your customers are being bombarded with marketing messages every day. Be persistent in your efforts to stay in front of your customers or you will get lost in the crowd. The best way to stay in front of your customers and make them feel good about you is by using lots of "quality touches." A "quality touch" is any communication your customer finds interesting, helpful, or entertaining. In other words, a quality touch is something they welcome in their inbox, mail box, or on their answering machine.

A quality touch can come in many, many different ways. It could be your regularly scheduled e-newsletter, it could be an invitation to your customer appreciation event, it could be a phone call telling them the new spring collection is in and you see a blouse you know your customer will love. The possibilities are endless. What's important is that the message makes people feel good about being your customer.

To use a quality touch you must have a legitimate reason to communicate. Here are some ideas that we expand on in this section.

- Give a great offer.
- Show them you care (holiday card, for example).
- Educate or inform them about something important.
- Send them messages that entertain them.
- Recognize their personal accomplishments.
- Send them an invitation.

Some of you can communicate with your customers frequently. For example, here at WhizBang! Training we communicate with our customers every week when we send out our WhizBang! Tip of the Week. Others will contact their customers only a few times a year. You may contact them more at some times of the year than others if you are in a seasonal business, during a new product launch, or if something particularly exciting is happening in your business.

Whatever your situation, give yourself a communication goal. How often do you want to get in touch with your customers? How many quality touches can you generate?

A Key Statistic—67 Percent   Here's a number that many of you have heard before, but it's so important that it bears repeating. Sixty-seven percent of customers stop shopping at a store or using a service because of "perceived indifference." Not because of price, selection, convenience, or service, they switch to your competition because *they think you don't care.* Your customers think you don't care whether they shop with you or not; they think you don't care about their business. Now, you may care passionately, but unless your customer knows about it, they perceive you as indifferent.

The good news is this: Logic dictates that if 67 percent of your customers are leaving because they think you don't care, then show them that you *do* care about their business, and they will remain your customers!

This is why it is so critical to keep your customer database up-to-date and to regularly communicate with everyone on it. Regular communication with your customers is the best way to make sure they know you care about them as a customer.

A schedule of at least four contacts a year is a bare minimum. This could include a holiday card and notifications of three promotions—but there are literally hundreds of reasons to communicate with your customers and many ways to reach them. It is your responsibility to be remembered by the customer, not their job to re-member you.

Key Concept #2: The Secret Strategy:
Become a Broader Resource

One of your challenges is to find genuine, authentic reasons to communicate with your customers. Information about your favorite new products or news about your latest promotions are fine, but if that's all you ever talk about, your customers will soon lose interest. They will stop reading your flyers and newsletters, and they will un-subscribe from your e-newsletter.

This is why you must expand the scope of your information and become a broader resource for your customers. Don't just tell them about you and your products; give them news and informa-tion that will make their lives better, solve their problems, or spark an interest. Here are four ways for you to become a broader resource.

1. *Become a Trusted Expert.* Hobbyists, like sewers, gardeners, fishermen, knitters, or kite fliers need someone they can trust for recommendations, information on products, and tips on becoming better at what they love to do. They have an almost insatiable de-sire for information. Communicating your expertise is a great way to establish yourself as *the* source for news and opinion.

The owner of a garden center could, as many of our clients do, have a Great Garden Tip that helps make gardening a more enjoy-able, rewarding experience. A bike store owner could write a newsletter (either paper or email) that keeps its readers up-to-date on the local bike scene. A pet store owner could give tips on better pet care.

Ask yourself the questions, "What do my customers ask me about when they come into my store? What interests them? What do they like about my store?" The answer to these questions will give you some insight into what they want to know about. You're probably already an expert; you just need to communicate your expertise to your customers. Of course, making sure they get all this valuable information is a wonderful reason to communicate regularly with them!

2. *Be a Clearinghouse for Information.* Another way to be a broader resource is to be a clearinghouse for information that affects your customers. If you are a toy store owner, you could be a parenting resource. You could have information about:

- Schedules at the local children's museum.
- Kids events at the Parks and Recreation Deparment.
- Reading clubs at the local library.
- Seminars on parenting.
- Family friendly restaurants.

If you are a bike store owner, you could be a resource to riders by distributing information about:

- Schedules of bike races in your area.
- The results of those races.
- Maps of bike trails.
- Links to other websites of other bike groups in your area.

If you are a custom framing gallery owner, you could connect your customers to the local art scene:

- Museum exhibits.

- Artists' websites.

- Area Arts Council information.

- Schedule of art classes by local artist.

An advantage of being a clearinghouse for information is that you don't have to create the content; you just have to distribute it, post it on your website, or put your customers in touch with people who can help them.

Ask yourself, "What would my customers find fun, interesting, or helpful?" When you've answered this question you know what kind of information you should make available.

3. *Deliver Gossip and Celebrity News.* When we talk about gossip we aren't referring to spreading malicious rumors. We're talking about "shop talk." Every community, off line or online, has its cast of characters, and news about these celebrities is interesting to members of the community.

Think of your church bulletin or a trade journal you subscribe to. It probably has news about people who have died, awards people have won, and other news of the community.

Many of your customers were drawn to you because, as specialty retailers, you created a sense of community among your customers—or because both you and your customers are part of a bigger community based around your interests.

At the Mackinaw Kite Co. we were part of a community of local kite fliers and many of us were part of the regional, national, and international kite community. Being tied into your communities and keeping everyone connected is a great way to build customer loyalty. Plus it gives you a great reason to stay in touch with your customers.

Be *the* place to go for information about what's happening in your community.

4. *Create a Place for Your Customers to Meet Each Other.* Putting a bulletin board up in your store and allowing your customers to ask questions, meet each other, and generally be part of a community is a wonderful and inexpensive way to show your customers that you want to be helpful. Although it is beyond the reach of most small retailers, having online chat or message boards for your customers is another great way to be a broader resource for your customers.

Of course, you can do all of these things—be the trusted expert, be a clearinghouse for pertinent information, be a community news source, and create meeting spaces. In fact, the more you do, the more deeply you'll connect with your customers.

Four Low-Tech Tactics to Get Your Customers to Shop More Often

The next four tactics are fun for your customers and profitable for you. What better combination could you possibly ask for? As you lavish lots of attention on your current customers they will reward you with their loyalty and their dollars.

Shop More Often Tactic #1: Have Lots of Promotions

Promotions can be flat out free or cost you a king's ransom. They can be done on the fly, taking almost no time or they can be the most time-intensive part of your business. It all depends on what you do. Promotions and special events are the salt and pepper in your marketing plan. They spice things up and keep your business fun and exciting. Promotions are a great way to keep your regular customers interested in your products and services and give them more reasons to shop with you every year. They can also give your customers a reason to keep shopping with you year, after year, after year.

There are lots of kinds of promotions and they could all have a place in your marketing plan. As you start choosing kinds of promotions and special events, think about the strategies you have identified for your business. Make sure your promotions support your strategy.

For example, if one of your company strategies is to be the expert resource, then educational classes, a lecture series, or hands-on training events are types of promotions that would support and strengthen your strategic position. If you want to be the most fun company in town, think parties galore, crazy contests, or extravagant festivals.

Price versus Value Added   When many small business owners think of promotions, they automatically think of putting goods and services on sale. This is one very successful type of promotion. Many of these promotion ideas go hand in hand with putting merchandise on sale. But there are also lots of great promotions that get their impact from fun and added value rather than cash savings. Try out both kinds and your customers will be twice as happy.

Here are a couple of the more popular types of strictly sale events.

Clearance Sales   For retailers, these are a necessary part of doing business and a great opportunity to get rid of old merchandise and generate cash to bring in new stuff for your next season. Have a small clearance section in your store all the time, but limit the number of truly price-based blowout sales to just a couple of times a year *max*. Otherwise your customers will never buy from you at full price.

Some types of clearance sales to consider are: Sidewalk Sales, End of Season Sales, Post Holiday Sales, End of Model Year Sale, or Discontinued Line Sale.

High-Season Sales　In this type of sale put your best merchandise on sale when you have the most people in the store, and work hard to move *tons* of it. Depending on your business, the high season may be anything from Mother's Day, to Christmas, to Fourth of July.

This type of promotional event is intended to motivate customers to buy from you rather than your competition when they are most inclined to buy. The problem is that small independent businesses can rarely compete with the enormous corporate competition in either price or advertising power. So the people who buy from you would likely have purchased from you anyway, and you're just losing margin.

There are ways to combat this problem and run successful high-season sales, however. I give you some of our favorite holiday promotions later in this section.

Value-Added Promotions　One reason people like to buy "on sale" (and there are many reasons) is because they like to get more for their money. So instead of lowering your price, give them more. *Add Value*.

When you add something *of real value* to your customer, you'll find that they won't need a discount in order to make the buying decision. In fact, you'll absolutely beat the low-price competition on that one sale—and could possibly wrap up a customer for life.

So think past the big *Sale* signs in your window and offer events that feature fun, education, or inspiration, *not discount*.

This type of promotional event, when done well, not only gives your customers an exciting reason to visit your store, but sets you up as an expert resource and encourages full-price buying.

They Did It ...

The owner of an East Coast tack shop created a fun promotion by sending her top 200 customers a mailing featuring a poem she wrote and a single fleece glove. To get the glove's mate her customers had to come into the store. Each package, including the glove and postage, cost her $3.40. More than 100 people (better than a 50 percent response rate!) came in and picked up their second glove. Her average sale for customers who came in was just over $76.

She said, "I love the fact that my best customers got a little special attention, but I really loved the fact that this promotion generated some badly needed cash during my off-season!"

... You Can, Too!

Some of these events may be so great that you may actually be able to charge for them and turn them into a profit center for your business. But don't feel you have to; the main idea is to get your customers into your business, get them excited about your product or service, get them to buy more often, and make them loyal, long-term customers.

Here is one sample idea (with many more to follow) for adding value. This specific idea is for the floral industry, but please, if you're not a florist, keep reading. Think about how you can translate this idea for your own business.

Valentine's Day is a big opportunity for florists to sell roses, but there is a ton of low-price competition: The big box grocery store has roses, Sam's Club has roses, the corner convenience mart has roses. Not to mention the competition from all the other professional florists in town.

So instead of selling roses at a lower price to make yourself stand out in the crowd, add something *of real value* to the gentlemen buying Valentine's Day roses for their wives, mothers, or girlfriends.

To do this, you've got to keep in mind that he isn't really buying roses but a romantic way to say, "I love you." Give everyone who buys a dozen roses for Valentine's Day a gift certificate redeemable in March for a single rose with a card attached that says, "Because Valentine's Day Isn't the Only Day I Love You Enough to Give You Flowers."

With one simple gesture you've made him a romantic hero, not just once (on Valentine's Day when it was expected), but twice (and the unexpected single rose is *ultraromantic*). Now *that's* added value.

Bonus to you: You get that guy back into your store one more time and he starts to think of you as the only place to buy flowers for his sweetheart (more transactions per year). While most of the guys will get their single rose and leave, some of them will buy more (higher average sale).

Double bonus to you: When the wife, girlfriend, or mother gets that unexpected single rose and is delighted, thrilled, and charmed at his thoughtfulness, your customer will start thinking about surprising her more often with flowers.

Triple bonus to you: Not everyone will actually come in to redeem their gift certificate, but you will have offered the extra value to everyone.

No question about it, finding and delivering something *of real value* to your customer takes more thought and perhaps more work than slapping a sale sign in your window, but the payback in significantly higher margins and customer loyalty is worth it.

Another Handful of Examples to Jump-Start Your Thinking
Don't get bogged down by the specific industries these examples are highlighting. Think about how you could adapt, change, or adjust the concept for your business. If you are doing all the same things

that everyone else in your industry is doing, you'll never achieve ultrasuccess. Very successful businesses look outside their industries and try to adapt best practices from others.

Health food stores could offer a series of healthy cooking classes by a local chef. One day might be gluten free cooking, next cooking with organic honeys, then 27 ways to add fiber to your food.

An outdoor adventure store might do a monthly movie night with documentary movies on mountain climbing, extreme kayaking, trekking in the Amazon, or walking the Appalachian trail. Highlight products similar to those used in the movies and let people try them out after the movie.

Women's clothing stores could offer evening events featuring minimakeovers like the ones you see on TV. Recruit makeup artists, personal shoppers, local salons and spas, or professional image consultants to donate services in exchange for publicity and access to your customers. Dress your customers in amazing outfits. Give free hair styling. Do makeup consultations. And offer before and after pictures.

A landscape designer or garden center could offer a citywide garden tour. Tour homes and businesses for which you have recently done landscaping to show off your best work. Print up a tour brochure that highlights the best design features and newest plants used in each location. Charter a bus. You could even sell tickets and donate a portion of the proceeds to a local garden club, land conservancy, or other appropriate charity.

A massage therapist could offer a workshop on gentle massage techniques parents can use on their children.

A financial planner or stock broker could hold an annual black tie event where partygoers bet on stock market style games (there are a *ton* of these; I searched Google under "Games about the Stock Market"). This kind of event teaches about good investing, gets people excited about investing, and sets you up as the expert. Donate money won by the "bank" to the local United Way or other charity.

An upscale bar and grill could have a guest bartender once a month on a usually slow night. Invite the mayor, the fire chief, local (or big name) celebrities, captains of industry, or colorful characters to come and tend bar for the evening. Name a drink and appetizer special after them for the evening, and watch them fly out the door!

Celebrate Famous Birthdays   This promotion is one of my favorites. This idea is fun for both you and your customers. Do it for a day, a week or a month. It all depends on how you celebrate. Here are some suggestions to get your brain juices flowing; the possibilities are endless.

- If you own a coffee shop, celebrate Bob Marley's birthday by selling Jamaican Blue Mountain coffee for $8 a pound instead of $12. Your customers will get hooked on the delicious flavor of your most expensive coffee.

- If you own a deli, celebrate the birthday of the Earl of Sandwich by giving away something special (a cookie? chips? drink upgrade? your store logo T-shirt?) with every sandwich ordered.

- If you own a bookstore, celebrate Gutenberg's birthday in a month-long promotion when you invite school kids in to learn about the printing press. Send press releases to the local newspapers; they'll eat it up and you'll get free publicity.

- If you own a high-end women's apparel store, celebrate Coco Chanel's birthday. Have a cocktail party and give away samples of her fragrances. Ask your local department store's perfume counter to donate the samples.

- If you own a lighting store or home center, celebrate Thomas Edison's birthday by giving away a free carton of four light bulbs with every purchase (get your vendor to donate them) or a discount on a lighting fixture that is overstocked.

You get the idea. Have fun coming up with your own ways to celebrate the birthday of a famous person who relates to your business. One tip: It's usually best to pick a dead famous person to celebrate; the live ones could get cranky about your using their names and birthdays.

Throw a Party   Throw a party to celebrate—whatever you can think of: Back to School pizza party, Anniversary of the First Man on the Moon party, St. Patrick's Day, a Super Bowl Party, a Star-Gazing party, a Cinco de Mayo party, an Arbor Day party (BYO picnic and plant a tree donated by the company), Beach Blanket Bingo party, an Oscars party, the Indy 500 party.

Holidays   I promised some of our favorite holiday promotions, and here they are.

Halloween   This holiday ranks second only to Christmas when it comes to consumer spending. Get your piece of the action even if you don't sell traditional Halloween stuff. Don't just give away candy in a plastic pumpkin; think about something easy and interesting you can do to get your customers into your store. Here's some food for thought.

- Offer Scary Savings on all black or orange clothing.
- Turn your stockroom into a haunted house for a night (as if it's not scary enough already) and invite your customers in for cider and popcorn.
- A florist might offer free bouquets of dead flowers tied with black ribbon—while supplies last. Or see if you can partner

with your local florist to give away the ghastly bouquets with their business card tied in the ribbon.

- Chiropractors can give away cheapie skeleton earrings to everyone who makes an appointment during the week of Halloween. Get earrings from a novelties catalog.

Easter   This promotional idea is tried and true. It combines the fun and suspense of a lottery with the chocolate and spring pastels of Easter—a winning combination!

Get a large basket and fill it with green Easter grass and 100 of those plastic eggs that come apart in two pieces. Into every egg put a chocolate egg or other Easter confection and a slip of paper with a percentage off.

After they have finished shopping, let your customer pick an egg, eat the candy, and get the discount on their entire purchase. If you don't want to offer this to the general public but want to reward your very best customers, send a postcard and have them trade it in for an egg. This is good because it lets you know which customers have responded to your postcard.

Christmas   You don't really have to do anything for this to be the biggest sales time of the year. But try this promotion to maximize your holiday sales.

Hold a Christmas Merchandise Preview the three weeks before Thanksgiving. Send a letter or postcard or announce it in your regular newsletter. Include three coupons: the first for 20 percent off the week three weeks before Thanksgiving (list dates on the coupon—learn from our mistakes), the second for 15 percent off two weeks before Thanksgiving, the third for 10% off the week before Thanksgiving.

This promotion accomplishes *several* very important things:

- It gets your customers in to shop with you early in the Christmas season when you need cash flow and they still have most of their Christmas budget to spend.

- It shows you early in the season what your best-sellers are so you can reorder while the vendor still has a supply of the hot item.

- It lets you know early what the real dogs are so you can mark them down early and have a chance to clear them out at a higher margin.

- It gives your customers a chance to buy early and then also to buy again later, say, about Christmas Eve. You know they will!

A great addition to this promotion is to give a bounce-back coupon to everyone who buys during the Christmas Preview inviting them back for 10 percent off the Friday, Saturday, and Sunday after Thanksgiving.

Informational/Educational Events   Seminars and classes are used to bring your regular customers in as well as to bring in prospects. Examples of this type of promotion are a seminar on Water Gardening for a garden center, a hair styling show featuring the latest styles, sewing lessons, demonstrations of the latest and greatest in hearing aid technology; you get the idea.

They Did It . . .

The owner of a popular New York City sewing store attributes much of his long-term success to a solid schedule of sewing classes.

"Our class schedule gives first-time buyers confidence that we are here to help them succeed. Our store becomes sort of a social center for our regular customers. They meet each other for lunch or dinner before class and of course they have lots of fun sewing together in class. This all keeps them coming back more often and puts us on the top of their list when it's time to get a new machine."

. . . You Can, Too!

Educational events can reinforce you and your staff as the experts in your field. Or you can bring in guest experts for even more panache. For example, we have a local outdoor outfitter who brought in one of the world's top climbers to give a lecture and slide presentation on his most recent Everest attempt.

Big Blowout Events   While this kind of promotion is not for everyone, it can be a *huge* plus for those of you willing to tackle a project of this scope. These kinds of big events make excellent Annual events that your customers will look forward to year after year. They can make you bulletproof against the soulless, corporate competition. Done correctly they can bring in amazing amounts of sales.

At the Mackinaw Kite Co. we held an annual kite festival that drew more than 65,000 people from all over the world for an exciting, action-packed, three-day event. The time and money involved with a promotion like this are significant. But we felt the investment was worthwhile because it always got photos on the cover of *at least* three regional newspapers, all the area TV stations covered the festival, it reinforced our position as a market leader in the kite world, and probably most importantly our customers *loved* it. It was great to invite our customers to this huge, fun party.

Oh, yeah, and we sold a gazillion kites at the very beginning of the season when we needed the cash.

Fun, Crazy Contests   Contests are an exciting way to get people to come into your store more often. *Here's one crazy idea*: Raffle off dinner with a celebrity.

Know someone famous? Or at least famous in their field? Or famous in your town? Is your second cousin Julia Roberts? Is your college roommate now a household name? See if they'll consent to have dinner with you and two of your customers.

Raffle off dinner for two with you and your celebrity. One

chance to enter every day. Be sure to use raffle tickets that have name and address on them so you can contact the winner—and add all the names to your customer mailing list! This is fun as well as great marketing. Send press releases about the contest to the local paper.

Here's another example of a fun promotion that was featured in our Tip of the Week. Buy two of the same jigsaw puzzle with a Valentine's Day theme. Or a Fourth of July theme. Or whatever theme works for your business or the time of year.

If you have 1,000 customers on your mailing list, buy puzzles with 1,000 pieces. If you have more customers on your list, buy bigger puzzles. I saw one with 18,000 pieces the other day! If the idea of putting together a puzzle this big boggles your mind, use a smaller puzzle, but buy enough so you have a piece to send each of your customers.

Put one of the puzzles together *minus one piece*, glue the completed puzzle to a foam core board, and display it in your store. Send a piece from the second puzzle to each of your customers, or a select group of your customers. Include an invitation to come into your store and see if they have the missing piece. If the piece they got in the mail is the missing piece from the puzzle displayed in your store, they're the winner!

What they win is up to you, but make it a really good prize or no one will bother to come check out their puzzle piece. How about a $100 shopping spree at your store? Cost to you is just $50—very cheap if you get lots of customers back shopping in your store. If you have tons of frequent flyer miles from going to trade shows, offer a free plane ticket anywhere in the continental United States. Now that's a good prize that costs you no cash at all. Remember: There is a chance that the customer with the missing puzzle piece will never make it into your store to claim their fabulous prize.

It's fun, it's easy, and it's different!

Here's an advanced angle you can try for this promotion: Team up with several other merchants in your downtown, street, or shopping area and each of you feature a different puzzle. Merge your customer lists and send your customers a piece from each puzzle. Your customers get more chances to win, you and your colleagues split the costs of the mailing, you will get a chance to get new customers, and you have an easy way to execute promotion for your entire shopping district.

Here's a high-tech version of this promotion to drive people to your website: Scan the puzzle with the missing piece and post the image on your website. Either have it hidden so people have to explore your site to find it, or post it on a page you really want them to see (new product info, for example), and send them directly to that page.

There. You see how an idea that at first blush seemed to be only for brick and mortar store owners can be adapted for all kinds of other businesses?

They Did It . . .

A Midwest florist did a variation of the jigsaw promotion with great success. He filled a treasure chest with enough goodies and gift certificates for flowers to make the contents extremely valuable. He mailed thousands of keys, one of which fit the chest, with the message, "If your key opens the treasure chest you get all the amazing stuff inside" and listed the contents of the chest.

He reported, "I couldn't believe the number of people who came in to try their key. Everyone had so much fun with it. Of course they all bought flowers while they were there. In fact, it was my best promotion ever!"

. . . You Can, Too!

Small, Low Overhead, Regularly Scheduled Promotions At the Mackinaw Kite Co. we always had a kite flyer on the beach on Tuesday nights to give lessons to anyone who was interested in talking to an expert. It cost us almost nothing, it was a benefit that our customers loved, and our professional kite fliers were trained to promote products and generate sales.

It's important to note that we usually had a kite flier on the beach every night, but because we billed Tuesday as Kite Night and promoted it as such, people felt more comfortable talking to the fliers and getting lessons. Labeling it as a promotion and encouraging people to participate led to a significant increase in participation.

Since it gets really, really cold here on the shores of Lake Michigan, Tuesday nights during the winter became the night for free yo-yo lessons—not kite flying. There are always a dozen kids or so who come into the store for lessons. And of course they need new string, the latest greatest yo-yos, instructional videos, and all the rest.

We have a knitting store client who has Sit 'N Knit Night. There's really nothing special planned. It's just a time when knitters can feel comfortable coming in and sittin', chattin', and knittin'. It's the modern day version of the quilting bee, I suppose. The customers love it and it keeps them coming into the store week after week. These people would never buy their knitting supplies anywhere else—even if it meant saving a couple of bucks.

Think of ways that you can incorporate easy to execute, regularly scheduled promotions or classes into your marketing plan.

To Sum It All Up Having a full, interesting, and varied schedule of promotions is one of the very best ways to keep customers coming into your store, to stay in touch with them, and to keep building great relationships.

Shop More Often Tactic #2: Have a Big, Bold, Preferred Customer Club

It doesn't matter whether you call it a preferred customer club, a frequent buyer program, or a rewards program, this tactic is a fantastic marketing tool for almost every retail store out there. Frequent buyer clubs, if administered correctly, reward your customers for their two most important shopping behaviors: *shopping often and spending lots.*

At its best, a frequent buyer club:

- Develops customer loyalty.
- Increases the number of times your customers shop with you.
- Increases your average sale.
- Builds your mailing list.
- Enhances your store's image and reputation.

This is an incredibly powerful combination of benefits.

Think about what this kind of program has done for the airlines. Almost everyone is signed up for a frequent flyer program with one of the airlines (the only thing you have to lose is a free ticket) and they create unbelievable loyalty. If you are a United Airlines frequent flyer, you'd never consider booking a trip on Northwest Airlines. And because you know that each purchase of airline tickets is getting you closer to that free trip, it takes the sting out of the high price tag. Great benefits for both the airlines and the customer.

Who Should Use a Frequent Buyer Program?   Almost every store can use some form of a frequent buyer program. In general, the more competition you have in your market, the more benefit you'll get from a frequent buyer club. The way you set up the program and the type of rewards given really depend on the type of store you have.

Frequent buyer programs work extremely well with stores whose customers shop often for their particular type of merchandise. These stores include:

- Stores that sell high-end commodities, such as food or clothing, that have certain features or benefits that justify a higher price. Examples include organic vegetables, high-quality vitamins and health products, or specialty children's clothing. The airline example I gave would probably fit into this category.
- Frequently visited food and drink establishments. Coffee shops, sandwich shops, and ice cream parlors.
- Stores that sell supplies for hobbyists. Pet stores, sewing stores, hobby shops, kite stores, photography stores, bike stores, knitting stores, boat stores, running stores, garden centers.
- Bookstores.
- Certain types of gift stores: toy stores, card shops, novelty stores, collectibles stores, and other gift shops with a narrow, well-defined market niche.

Please realize that this is just a partial list. You may find that although your store does not fit any of these categories, a frequent buyer program may still be a wonderful service for your customers.

Conversely, your store may perfectly fit one of these categories, but because of certain other factors (for example, 85 percent of your customers are tourists), a frequent buyer program may not be the best marketing tool for you.

A frequent buyer is less likely to work for the following types of stores, although some kind of program (and we've listed one) could probably work *even in these situations.*

- Stores selling luxury, prestige items such as furs, high-end original art, couture fashions, high performance sports cars.
- Stores where the product line has an extremely long life cycle, such as an appliance store. People purchase a washer and dryer only once every decade or so. A frequent buyer program isn't likely to stimulate people to buy more major appliances so they can get a discount.

What Kind of Program Would Be Best for Me?   There are four basic kinds of programs to consider.

1. *Program Style #1.* The first, and our favorite, style of program rewards your customers for shopping often and buying lots.

Let me tell you a little bit about my experience. I always buy my books at our local, independent bookstore. They have a program built into their point of sale system that automatically spits out a coupon for a $10 credit every time you spend $100.

I salivate every time I stand at that register. And when I get that coupon, I feel like I've won the lottery. Even though I could buy books for less at a big chain or online, I always shop at this store. Why? Because it's fun, it rewards me for being a frequent customer (rather than lures me with price), and every time I get a coupon it cements our relationship a little more.

Well, I decided our store had to have a similar frequent buyer program. I spent quite a bit of time researching the available computerized options, but everything I found was either too complicated and/or too expensive. And it was too complicated to track by hand how many hundred dollar units the customer had purchased. It was very frustrating.

One day I came into the store and my brother and partner, Steve, exclaimed, "I've figured out our frequent buyer program!" With this system you have a club card for each customer (this can be as simple as the back of your business card) and the total amount of the customer's purchase before tax is recorded in a space on the card. It looks something like this:

Name:	*Ms. Susie Smith*	
$ 24.99	$86.04	$12.99
$125.68		

After your customer has filled the card, the total dollars spent is added up and the card becomes a gift certificate good for 10% of the total dollars.

Although many people use 10 purchases before giving the coupon, we recommend 6. Why? Because it gives you the opportunity to reward the customer more often. The number you use depends on your business and how often a customer normally shops with you. Remember: Your goal is to get the customer in to shop with you more frequently.

I think this system is even better than the bookstore system I described because it encourages repeat visits as well as a higher average sale. The customer knows they'll get rewarded after six purchases and they also know that the more they buy, the more money they'll get back.

2. *Program Style #2.* The second kind of program is the "buy 10, get 1 free" kind of club. This type of program works very well if you have a single inexpensive product that your customers buy

very frequently or there is a lot of competition for your customer's business.

The Cricket Club is a perfect example of this kind of club. One of our clients has a pet store. They were losing their cricket business to the lower cricket prices at a big box pet store chain up the road. Not only were they losing their cricket business, but they were losing the extra business that came when the owners of iguanas, toads, and other cricket-consuming pets shopped for their crickets.

Rather than concede the cricket business or lower their prices, they started a frequent buyer club—the Cricket Club. Buy 10 dozen crickets and get the next dozen free. Their cricket business went through the roof, margins remained high, and, most importantly those customers walk through our client's door every week, not the competition's.

Coffee shops and delis also do very well with this kind of club. Customers spend bucks on coffee and lunches every day; the trick is to get them to spend them most frequently with you. The card for this kind of club might look like this. You'll probably need an unusual shaped punch, a hard-to-copy ink stamp, or have your employees initial each box so your customers aren't tempted to x right through all their spaces on their own.

```
┌─────────────────────────────────────────────────────┐
│  Name:    Ms. Susie Smith                            │
│                                                       │
│       ⊠    ⊠    ┌─┐  ┌─┐  ┌─┐                         │
│       1    2    │3│  │4│  │5│                         │
│                 └─┘  └─┘  └─┘                         │
│     ┌─┐  ┌─┐  ┌─┐  ┌─┐  ┌──┐                          │
│     │6│  │7│  │8│  │9│  │10│                          │
│     └─┘  └─┘  └─┘  └─┘  └──┘                          │
└─────────────────────────────────────────────────────┘
```

The number of items the customer needs to buy depends on your business and how often an average customer currently buys from you. Ten works well for something that your customer might buy once or twice a week.

3. *Program Style #3*   The third kind of program is good for higher ticket merchandise that your customer might shop for only occasionally, like clothing or home accessories. It focuses on getting your customer into your store on a regular basis.

In this program offer your customer an incentive to come in and buy each month. For example, give them 20 percent off a single item one time a month. If you're doing your job, they will leave with one item they got at a discount and several others they purchased at full price. The club card might look like this:

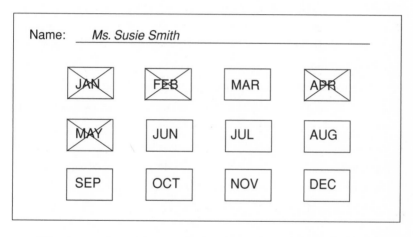

This type of program really lends itself to personal service. If you keep track of the customers in the club, you'll be able to call or email everyone who hasn't been in that month around the twentieth and invite them in to use their discount for the month and see your newest merchandise.

Consider tracking each customer to see how much they buy with each month's discount and how the discount is spread across the whole purchase. For example, a customer might buy a blazer with her 20 percent off and the skirt, pants, scarf, and blouse to match at regular price. The discount on the total sale might add up to only 8 percent!

4. *Program Style #4*   This fourth style of frequent buyer program is one that would work for high-end, luxury, or long-life cycle products or services. In this style of program reward your customer when they have purchased a specified "set" of your products.

In the appliance store example I mentioned the customer not needing to buy more than one washer and dryer every decade or so. True. Instead, encourage them to buy any and all appliances from you. Give a rebate (or some other bonus) if a customer buys any four of the following six appliances from you within five years: washer, dryer, dishwasher, fridge, garbage compactor, oven.

A furrier might offer a free fur-trimmed hat when a customer has purchased a full-length coat, a jacket-length coat, and either a fur shawl or vest.

A landscaping company might offer some bonus for customers using all four: garden maintenance program, lawn care program, lawn mowing service and, snow plow service.

A science and technology company may want to offer incentives for customers who purchase multiple products or who sign up in advance for product upgrades.

The idea of all of these programs is to encourage your customers to buy more frequently from you (even if that means once every three and a half years instead of once every five years) and also to choose your products and services over all their other spending options.

The Nitty-Gritty Details of Putting the Program in Place

Here is the "how-to" along with the tips, tricks, and techniques we've found that really make your frequent buyer program a big success.

Name Your Program   This is usually fun. Be creative. Examples include our clients with the Cricket Club, or an ice cream shop named Sweet Temptations that has a Sweethearts Club. If you can't think of a good, original name, go with the old standby, (Your store's name's) Rewards Program or Preferred Customer Club.

Determine Your Policies and Procedures

Make these decisions:

1. What style of program will you offer? How many purchases do customers have to make before they can redeem their prize? What will they get for free? What kind of discount will they get?

2. What additional benefits will club members receive? Remember: Everyone loves the sense of belonging, of being special. What other benefits can you offer your club member other than the 10 percent discount or the free dozen crickets? Free delivery on Tuesdays? Club member newsletter? Special sales for members only? A travel mug with your logo on it? Free workshops?

    See Figure 3.1 for the list that one of our clients has posted on her website that explains the benefits of her preferred customer club.

3. How you will track the customer's purchases? Will you use a card or keep the information on a spreadsheet? You can custom design a card, use a business card, or use a simple recipe card.

4. Will you keep the cards at the store, make the customer carry them, or give them a choice? There are pluses and minuses to both methods.

    If you keep the cards at your store, organized alphabetically in a recipe box at the counter, you have control of the program. And it eliminates the problem of customers forgetting their cards, filling out a new one for each purchase or worst of all, just not participating because it's too big a hassle to bring in their card. However, if the customer keeps the card in their wallet, your store name is in front of their eyes every time they open the wallet up. This also puts the ownership of the program in the customer's hands and those who do participate are likely to be very good customers.

What are the benefits of being a member?

1. *Benefit #1*—Enrollment into our frequent buyer program. Once you become a member you will receive a *Bali Hai Club* card with 6 boxes on the back of it. Each time you make a nondiscounted purchase, whether on our website or in our store, the amount of your purchase (minus tax) will be entered into one of the squares. Once all of the squares are filled, you turn your card in and receive a gift certificate worth 10% of the combined total of all of your purchases.

2. *Benefit #2*—A chance every month to be entered into our drawing to win a $50 Shopping Spree!

3. *Benefit #3*—Advance notice of new shipments arriving from Bali so you can have the first pick of our newest merchandise.

4. *Benefit #4*—A free subscription to *Bali Update*, a weekly newsletter delivered direct to your inbox featuring news and events in Bali and surrounding Asia.

5. *Benefit #5*—An invitation to our annual party in March to celebrate the Balinese New Year. We close for Nyepi, a day of silence in Bali, to mark down items and then open the following day for members only. The party features food, fun, and most importantly great discounts exclusively for *Bali Hai Club* members.

Become a member of the *Bali Hai Club* and begin reaping the benefits today!

Note: Our privacy policy regarding your email address or any other information that you provide to us is that we will never sell, give away, or disclose any of your personal information—*period*!

Figure 3.1   Sample Member Benefits.

Invite Your Customers to Join the Club   How will you let customers know about the club and invite them to join? Signs in the store? A direct mail piece? Good ideas. And in addition, I recommend that your store standard is to ask every customer at the point of sale if they would like to participate in the program. The operative word is, ask. It is certainly fine if a customer doesn't want to participate, and your employees should be very gracious if a person isn't interested, but they should ask each customer if they would like to join.

Create a Sign-up Form   The sign-up form should, at the minimum, give your customers the basic program details you just outlined and get your customers' names and addresses for your mailing list. If you can do more, great. The more information (within reason) you can gather and give on no more than one page, the better.

Send a "Welcome" Letter   The same week a customer signs up for the first time, they should get a "welcome to the club" letter or postcard. It should thank them for signing up and reiterate the benefits of being a club member. If you sign them up and do nothing, chances are that a large number of your customers will just plain forget about it.

Train Your Staff   A great way to get your employees excited about the program is to have them help you plan it in the first place. Besides, they are the closest to your customers and will probably have some really great ideas that your customers will love.

When you have all the policies, procedures, and materials in place and ready to go, have a short staff meeting to introduce the program and lay out your expectations about how it will run. In the meeting review:

- The reason for the program.
- How it works.
- The benefits for the customer.
- Their role and responsibilities.
- What to do when something goes wrong (like a card gets lost).

Get It Going

Start reaping the rewards. It really is as simple as that. As with any other good program you must make a commitment to executing it, maintaining it, and nurturing it. But, done correctly, a frequent buyer program can be one of your most powerful tools.

They Did It . . .

The owner of an eclectic gift shop featuring dried flower arrangements started a Rewards Program and within one year had more than 900 active members.

He sent each new member a handwritten thank-you card, which contained two $5 gift certificates—one for the new member to use themselves and one to give to a friend.

They report that the average sale from these gift certificates is $70. Not only did the certificate generate a profitable sale, it brought them back into the store sooner. When asked to rate the program on a scale of 1 to 10 the owners rated it an 11!

. . . You Can, Too!

Shop More Often Tactic #3: Send Snail Mail

Sending your customers mail that is interesting, fun, or helpful is a wonderful way to get them to shop with you more often. Notice I didn't say junk mail. Direct mail, sometimes known as junk mail, involves sending mail to hundreds of thousands of people who have never heard of you before. Most of you reading this book don't have the expertise or the resources to get into the direct mail game.

What we're talking about here is putting mail into the mailbox of your current customers. As you have probably guessed, we love email as a marketing tool, but it will never completely replace what many affectionately call "snail mail."

Even if you become an expert with your email marketing we still recommend at least two hard-copy mailings a year—and four would be better. Some of you will be able to send a mailing every month and still get a positive return from every mailing. If this is true for you, don't stop mailing!

Postcards Postcards are great because they possess a powerful marketing one-two punch: They are inexpensive and because you don't have to open an envelope they almost always get read. Postcards are the cheapest piece of mail you can send.

Hot Tip!

There are several "on demand" services that will print and send postcards and greeting cards. You can use their designs or download your own. It's a wonderful way to send mailings that are too big to label and stamp yourself, but too small to justify hiring out to a mailing house.

To learn more about some of these services go to the Retailer Resources page of our website: www.whizbangtraining.com.

Postcards are great for easy-to-understand messages like invitations to your promotions, your clearance sales, your customer parties. They also make great reminders for important events that people need to purchase gifts for, like Valentine's Day, Mother's Day, or Secretaries Day.

Send a simple postcard with a single helpful tip to all your customers. It would take a lot less time to produce than a newsletter, cost less to send, and would still be a valuable relationships building gesture.

Newsletters   Newsletters are powerful marketing tools. They give you an opportunity to tell your customers about all the cool things you do, all the great stuff you carry, and all the reasons why they should shop with you.

Newsletters are fantastic for positioning you as the trusted expert. Include articles or give tips that relate to your products. Research topics that are important or interesting to your customers. Make your newsletter bigger and more interesting than just your store.

Newsletters can be fun or funny, serious and compelling, cutting edge, or comfy-cozy. Make sure the tone and content matches your strategies.

There is one problem with newsletters. Most small and mid-sized store owners are too busy to produce a printed newsletter on a regular basis. Start with a quarterly piece and then increase as it gets easier for you to do. Don't start it if you are not 100% sure you can get it out regularly and to your standards. If you make a commitment to producing a newsletter, keep it.

Catalogs   Of course if you have a merchandise catalog, you will want to send it to your customers. Catalogs are sales tools and a good one will make you money.

However, catalogs don't usually have much value as a relationships building tool. Which is why we recommend you "soup up" your catalog and make it a magalog.

Magalog   Magalogs are part magazine, part catalog. They are a wonderful way to be a resource and sell stuff at the same time. A gourmet gifts store could print recipes and articles demonstrating cooking techniques on the same page as the cooking utensils needed for that particular recipe. An outdoor outfitter could put "staff picks" for favorite hiking trails next to a page featuring hiking shoes. A bookstore could publish "summer favorites" with staff reviews.

If you list lots of resources in your magalog, your customers will hang on to it longer, which, of course, increases the chances they'll buy from it.

At the Mackinaw Kite Co. we printed our magalog, *The Flyer*, on newspaper stock. It was incredibly inexpensive to print so we were able to make a ton of them, send them to all our customers, plus give them away to everybody in the store without worrying about the cost. Some of you, because of the type of merchandise you carry, may have to create a more expensive, upscale piece. The choice is yours. The important thing is that, in addition to selling your products, your magalog is relevant and interesting to read.

Using a Mailing Service   Using a mailing service can be an absolutely wonderful solution to getting out large mailings. A mailing house can print, fold, stuff, address, and stamp your direct mail piece—much faster and more often for far less money than you could do it yourself! And who needs the paper cuts and sticky stamp tongue?

If you plan to do a lot of direct mail, shop around, find a good mailing service that you trust, and build a strong relationship. These folks can really help you out.

A Word of Caution About Direct Mail   Don't let perfection get in the way of progress. If you can't consistently produce a full-blown newsletter or create a 30-page magalog on time, then just get something done and get it out there, even if it's a simple postcard or a 1-page tip sheet. The idea is to communicate frequently with your customers to boost sales and cement your personal relationships.

At the Mackinaw Kite Co. we spent months and months creating a beautiful yo-yo catalog. Unfortunately, by the time we finally got the darned thing printed, the yo-yo craze had nearly ended. Anyone want a slightly outdated yo-yo catalog? I think there are probably boxes of them still floating around somewhere.

Shop More Often Tactic #4: Use Bag Stuffers and Bounce Backs

Whether they are down and dirty or deluxe, bag stuffers are an easy way to communicate to your current customers and encourage them to visit again soon. In fact, this opportunity is just too good to miss!

Be sure to send your customers home with something that informs, entertains, sells, enlightens, or explains. It could be your schedule of events, one of your special reports, a tip sheet, a fun list of great gifts by age or type of person, a list of recommended resources, a sales letter for one of your newest products, or an invitation to your next special event.

Your bag stuffer could be your 18-page magalog, a 1-page flyer, a trifold, a quarter of a page, a note card, an audio CD. The possibilities are limited only by your imagination.

One great bag stuffer idea is a "bounce back," where you give customers a coupon or gift certificate for products or services that complement the ones they have just purchased. It's like add-on selling after the sale! And hopefully it bounces them back into your store.

For example:

- If the customer buys water plants from you, give them a coupon for water conditioning chemicals.
- If they buy a guitar, put a coupon for sheet music into the bag.
- If they buy a paperback book, put in an incentive to come back and buy a hardcover book.
- If they buy a business suit, put in a gift certificate for 10 percent off a dress shirt.

Think of ways you can make your bag stuffer stand out. Make sure the customer sees what you're stuffing!

Make it stand out visually:
- Fold heavy stock paper over note card style.
- Use brightly colored (but not ugly) papers.
- Cut-out shapes.
- Use large, extra bold fonts.

Make it stand out physically:
- Glue a piece of penny candy on your stuffer.
- Stick a pencil with your store logo through it.
- Put it inside a tiny box.
- Roll it up and tie it with raffia.

Have your employees show the customer the stuffer and tell them what they are putting into the bag. "I'm putting this article with 14 pruning tips for perennials in your bag—and there's a gift certificate for $5 off our best quality pruning shears, so don't throw it away!" Make sure the customer sees it going into the bag.

This technique is so darned simple there's no reason that everyone isn't doing it. In its simplest form all it takes is a little bit of imagination, some paper, and a printer.

Four High-Tech Tactics to Get Your Customers to Shop More Often

These are high-tech versions of the tried-and-true tactics in the previous sections.

Shop More Often Tactic #5: Manage Your Customer Database

All of the strategies and tactics to get your customers to shop with you more often assume you can easily communicate with them. Call it your mailing list, call it your customer list, call it your contact list, call it Fred if you want to. No matter what you call it, this collection of names, addresses, email addresses, and other pieces of customer information can be an extremely valuable asset for your business.

However, without all the customer contact information in one place it becomes difficult, if not impossible, to manage the process of communicating with your customers. Names you can't use aren't valuable at all.

We know many retailers who have stacks of guest books sitting around gathering dust filled with the names and addresses of years' worth of customers. Bob had a friend in Mackinaw City who had dozens of garbage bags filled with names on slips of paper collected from entries for a daily drawing. None of these names were worth more than the paper they were written on because they weren't easy to manage and consequently were never used.

Which is why it is critical to your future success to take your collection of names and create a customer *database*. A database is defined as "a large collection of information organized for rapid search and retrieval."

You can spend a huge amount of time and tens of thousands of dollars building and managing your database but most small to mid-sized retail store owners don't need this level of sophistication. In fact, we recommend that you use the old military acronym KISS— keep it simple, stupid. You want a clean list that is easy to use.

Here are a few things to consider when you create your database.

Keep the Right Information At the minimum have your customers' names, addresses, and email addresses. Don't forget the email address! After those basics carefully consider what type of customers you have, what type of marketing you plan to do, and how you plan on using your list.

If your product is pretty straightforward, say ice cream, you won't need anything more than basic contact information. However, many of you will want to develop customer profiles so you can send more specific messages to specific segments of your mailing list. A profile indicates a specific interest or buying pattern.

Examples of profiles are:

- Customers who have made a high dollar purchase.
- Customers who have taken a class or belong to a club sponsored by your store.
- Hot prospects.
- Customers who are interested in specific types of merchandise in your store, for example, mountain bikers, road racers, BMX bikers, family/kids bikers.

Be careful about overdoing it. There is a tendency to overestimate the amount of information you'll actually use. Be honest with yourself and don't create a database that is filled with lots of useless information. If you're not going to use it, there is no point in gathering it and managing it.

Find the Right Technology   Once again: Keep it simple. Have all the information in one place that is easy to manage. If it can't be managed, it won't be used. If you don't use it, you won't make any money with it.

Here are a couple of options to consider:

- Use the customer database function in your POS system—the best option.
- Enter the names in a simple spreadsheet like Microsoft Excel.
- Use a more sophisticated database like ACT or Goldmine.
- Use a database that is incorporated into your email marketing application like the database in WhizBang! Email—a must-do for email marketing.

A good system will allow you to sort information in your database by profile to send (via postal service or email) tightly focused messages. For instance a bike shop could send a postcard promoting its big race just to a profile named "race participants" or it could combine two profiles and send the mailing to everyone who fit the profiles "race participants" and "road bike purchasers," provided they had created those particular profiles, of course.

By not sending messages or postcards to everyone on the list, just the ones who are most likely to be interested, you cut down on your mailing costs and get more profitable results from your effort. As the size of your database increases, you can buy more sophisticated technology and hire professionals to help you manage the information, but get it computerized now. Don't let perfection get in the way of progress!

Enter Names Immediately   Lots of people have started gathering names with the best intentions, only to have the process fall apart within a few short weeks. This usually occurs because the process behind the project wasn't thought through properly.

However, the process is quite simple. There are two questions you need to answer: Who is responsible for entering the information and when are they going to enter it?

The best solution is to use your POS database and have your employees enter the information at the point of sale. Using your POS also has the advantage of tracking all your customers' purchases automatically so you can send specific merchandise targeted messages.

If you're collecting names manually—through a guest book sign-up, a preferred customer registration card, or slips of paper for a contest like our Mackinaw City friend, figure out how to get that contact information into a computerized format.

We strongly recommend you either schedule someone specifically to do the data entry or you hire outside help to do it. Having your staff on the floor try to do it when things are slow in the store is a recipe for disaster. It rarely gets done. Temp agencies are a great solution. They will send someone who is prescreened and qualified to enter lots of names quickly and accurately.

Bottom line: Figure out how you're going to make it happen, then do it.

Keep Your Mailing List Clean   Make sure that the information on your list is current and accurate so that most of your mail makes it to your intended recipient. You pay hard-earned cash every time you send something in the mail, so keeping your list clean saves you money and increases the return on your investment.

Here's a simple way to keep your list clean: At least once a year do a first class postcard mailing with the instruction Address Correction Requested printed next to the spot where you put the stamp. We recommend that you check with your post office for the most up-to-date rules on where to put the Address Correction Requested before you do your first cleanup mailing. Since you (1) sent them first class and (2) requested an address correction, the post office will return any undeliverable postcards to you with the reason it wasn't delivered and with a forwarding address if there is one.

Take these returned postcards and use the information to update your database. If there is a new forwarding address, change the address in your database; if there is no new address, delete that address.

Another way to keep your list clean is to run it through National Change of Address (NCOA) software before you send it. It updates any addresses that have registered a change of address with the U.S. Postal Service. That way more of your mail will be delivered in the first place. Find out more about this option at the U.S. Postal Service website www.usps.com. There is a whole section on their website about sending direct mail. If you use a mailing service to send your direct mail, they may also offer this NCOA service.

Changing your home address does not necessarily mean changing your email address. If you have the available resources and you get a postcard back with no forwarding address, you can send an email requesting an address correction.

Because people change email addresses frequently it can be very difficult to keep your email database up-to-date. Every week when we send out our WhizBang! Tip of the Week we get several "undeliverables." These emails went to the mailbox of the intended recipient, but the account was closed so it was bounced back, sent back to us with a message that it couldn't get through.

It's nearly impossible to track down what the new email address is. We feel it is not a good use of our resources to try. We imagine the same would be true for you. What we try to do instead is make our Tips so useful and informative that they are missed, and the recipient is prompted to find us and sign up with their new email address.

Think of Your Customer List as Business Insurance   Have you ever watched a national chain store open in your town and think "I sure hope that doesn't drive so and so out of business"? It's happened in our town several times in the past year. A big franchise marine store opened up two minutes from the local fellow. A new-concept ice cream franchise and a Starbucks opened just up the street from the local java joint and ice cream parlor. Home Depot opened directly across the street from the local hardware store.

The chain comes in, builds a shiny new store, spends enormous amounts of money on advertising, has a gala grand opening, and without a list of all their heretofore loyal customers, all the local merchant can do is sit around and watch as their customers switch to the new competition. If they don't have a great customer database, they have to be incredibly creative, spend tons of money to compete, or hope.

If that local business owner has a large and active database, they can fight back. They can communicate with their customers, remind them of all the benefits of shopping with their store, invite them to their fun events, and tell them they want to keep them as a customer.

Their customers may go try out the new national chain—who wouldn't? But if the local merchant plays to their biggest competitive advantage, their existing, meaningful relationships, their customers will be back. And probably spend more than ever.

It could be argued that your inventory is your most valuable asset or if you own your building that your real estate is your most valuable asset, but we beg to differ. Your customer database, that list with names, addresses, and email addresses, is your most valuable asset. Without a customer database you are merely a location with inventory. With a customer database you have the power to build relationships and build your business.

Shop More Often Tactic #6: Use Email Marketing to Stay in Touch with Your Customers

This tactic—using email marketing to stay in touch with your customers—is probably the most powerful and the most underused tactic for deepening and strengthening relationships with your customers. Done correctly, there is really no better way. Why?

Quite simply, email is the cheapest, easiest, and fastest way to stay in touch with your customers:

- *Cheap.* Almost any message you decide to send to your customers via snail mail can also be sent via email, and you avoid the printing, materials, and postage costs. It's definitely a big savings.

- *Easy.* Sending an email is easier than sending regular mail, too. You don't have all the hassle of designing, printing, stuffing, stamping, and hauling. All you do is write your message and click send.

- *Fast.* No more waiting around for the mail carrier to deliver your letter. When you send it, it gets there immediately. This is great if you have time-sensitive offers, like a special price good only through the end of next week.

Here's one of the biggest plusses with email: Your customer has an *easy, immediate* way to respond to you. All they have to do is hit Reply or *click a link to your website.* They don't have to decide to pick up the phone, they don't have to put anything into the mail, and they don't have to wait for regular business hours.

All this adds up to one thing. You can—and are much more likely to—communicate frequently with your customers and as a result you'll get stronger, deeper, better customer relationships.

In the rest of this section, you get some great ideas for how to use email marketing, what to do and what *not* to do, and some techniques to make your email messages more powerful and profitable.

The most important thing you can do right now—even if you don't want to use this tool immediately—is to *start gathering the email addresses of every customer, every prospect, every professional contact you have.* That way, when you start using this tool later (and you will), you'll have a list of addresses ready to go.

How to Use Email Marketing   There are so many wonderful ways to use email marketing to communicate to your customers. Here are just a few things you can consider as you develop your email marketing campaign.

Establish Yourself as the Expert   Email is a great format for sending out a weekly or monthly tip, article, or idea—something that will position you in the mind of your customer as an Expert.

Try a Great Gardening Newsletter, a Cleaning Tip of the Month, Hair Style Hints, or a Scrapbook Technique Tip. Give your customers valuable information that makes them want to read your newsletter and keeps your company name in front of them. If you become the Expert in their minds, they will automatically go to your store when they need your kind of goods or services. It's a great way to differentiate yourself from your competition.

They Did It ...

The owner of a Mid Atlantic state garden center reports she always features a particular plant in her email newsletters—a "plant of the month" if you will. She sees a sharp increase in the sales of the featured plant without discounting it at all.

She reports, "Initially I thought I would have to put the plants on sale to make the offer attractive, but I've learned that giving my customers some information and my recommendation is enough to bring them in for that particular plant."

... You Can, Too!

The other benefit of being an expert resource is that it improves the chances that your email will actually get read. If all you ever do is make a sales pitch or tell about your store, your customers will quickly stop reading and start deleting your email messages. If you give them information they are truly interested in, they will keep reading—and even look forward to your emails!

Inform Your Customers about Changes That Affect Them   Email is an easy way to get the nitty-gritty details about your business out to your customers. If you hire a new designer, let your customers know. If your fax number changes, blast out an email. If you are extending your store hours for the holiday season, get the word out. It's important information—plus it's one more communication from you that keeps your name at the top of your customer's mind.

In fact, these short informative emails can be an excellent "reminder" to your customer, and you'll frequently see a bump in sales even if you didn't make a single sales pitch or promote any of your events.

Notify Your Customers about Sales, Special Events, and Promotions   Pretty much any kind of promotion, sale, special event that you would notify your customers about through direct mail can be sent via email. It's even better to inform your customers *both* ways.

One of the best uses of email marketing I've ever seen is the nonprofit Land Conservancy group here on the Michigan lake shore. They send emails every week or two inviting their members and other interested people to all kinds of events: docent-led nature walks, site cleanup events, slide shows at local libraries, bird watching during the annual migrations, fundraising dinners, and so much more.

Because they are a nonprofit group, there's no way they could afford to send a piece of direct mail to every member, but email makes it easy to encourage participation and community involvement.

Generate Immediate Interest in Your Products or Services   If you have a slow period, or if you get in a big order of new items, the immediate nature of email is perfect to fill up your store fast. These are generally more off-the-cuff emails but can still be very successful.

There are two tricks: One is to make sure your message puts the "law of scarcity" into play ("one day only" or "for the first 27 customers" or "just three more ultra widgets left"). This makes taking action an urgent priority. The second is to give them a special offer if they do take action quickly.

This example does both:

My pain is your gain—UPS dropped off 47 boxes of new holiday merchandise today and I don't have quite enough room for all this great new merchandise in the store. So to make extra room, I'm offering you a special two-day deal. On these two days *only*, get 25% off any widget in the store plus I'll throw in a bottle of Widget Wax as a special thank-you."

They Did It . . .

A frame shop in Pittsburgh, Pennsylvania, sent an email trumpeting their "Steelers-Mania" promotion as soon as the Pittsburgh Steelers football team won the Super Bowl.

They went out and bought 50 special edition newspapers the day after the game to frame and make available to their customers. One of the owners commented, "Not only did we sell the framed newspapers, we framed other Steelers memorabilia for several months afterward. In addition, the more masculine display windows that we featured in our email blast attracted lots of new business from men. All in all, it was a great promotion that didn't take much time or money."

. . . You Can, Too!

One of our clients with a hobby store sends emails the day hot new merchandise arrives. He sends the message in the morning and figures that on average at least 10 people will show up by noon. How'd you like to be able to whip up immediate sales like that?

Make Time-Sensitive Offers   Email messages are very effective for perishable items like flowers or foods or for any weekly/daily specials that are available for only a short period.

Emailing the daily lunch specials to nearby businesses at about 11:00 as tummies are starting to growl would be a great way for restaurants to build their lunch clientele.

If you have a weekly flower special, email your list the day before it arrives to generate interest and remind people to stop in for their fresh bunch. You could even send a gorgeous picture of the flower in the body of the email.

Drive Customers to Your Website   Email is the best way for small businesses to drive customers to their website to buy products or to book appointments. Not search engines. Not reciprocal links. Nothing else works as well as communicating via email to your current customers and including links to your website.

When you include a link in your email, your website is only a simple click away. There's no typing. There's no searching. There's no remembering the web address. Emailing a link makes it bonehead simple for your customers to visit your site. Just click. You've taken away all possible barriers, so you'll get a lot more visitors.

Your link can go to your website home page if the invitation is general:

"Learn more about what's happening at Susie's Spokes on our website."

Or you can link directly to a specific page that relates to the message:

"Just click here for complete information on this do-it-yourself paint stripping kit."

If you're not sure how to put a link in your email or don't know how to turn a word or image into a "hyperlink," you should learn. It's very easy and extremely effective. Try to include a link to your website in every email you send. Get your customers used to visiting your site frequently.

Some Real-Life Examples   The best email messages combine one, two, or more of the elements just described. If you never give your customers something of interest, they will stop reading your messages; if you never make a pitch, you'll never increase your sales. The best email marketing does both: highlights a problem, a need, a desire that your customer may have, then tells them how they can fix it or get it, and positions your store as the best place to shop.

Figures 3.2 and 3.3 show actual emails sent by two of our Marketing Mentor Program clients. Check out how different the two formats are, but they both accomplish the same mission.

Bookworks Is Here!!!
This new line by Rebecca Sowers is something you've *got* to see.
There are spiral albums, accordion albums, and mailable card albums.
Rebecca has taken all the work out of making mini albums! The papers
and embellishments for Bookworks are fun and graphic, in brights or
pastels. Once you see the example, you'll want to try one on your own!

**Learn the Basics or Improve Your Skills with the
"Scrapbook Design University" on March 18 & 19**
Here's your chance to get some motivation or learn some new skills.
The Scrapbook Design University series of classes lets you choose
just the classes you want—or take the whole series—to get a solid
understanding of scrapbooking fundamentals. These classes are
enjoyable and affordable. Only $10 each! Sign up for the whole
series and pay only $40, plus get 20% off your purchases for the
weekend. Can't beat that!!

(Continued)

Figure 3.2   **Sample Email.**

Call to sign up 800-555-4327 or check out our website for <u>class information</u> and <u>online registration</u>.

Amazing March Special—Win a Shopping Spree!
The newsletter is in the mail, but in case you get yours late, here's part of the scoop: Spend $100 during March and we'll enter you into a drawing for a $100 gift certificate. You could win $100 of FREE SCRAPBOOKING SUPPLIES!

What's better? Every time you spend $100 during March, we'll enter you in the drawing. Spend $300, get three chances to win! You have all month to enter. All you have to do is save your receipts and when they total $100, bring them in and exchange them for an entry ticket. We'll draw the winner on April 1, and if we call you, it won't be an April Fool's joke!

Tip of the Week—Make Your Own Shadow Stamps
Shadow stamps are plain-shaped stamps without much detail. You stamp a shadow stamp in a light color, then stamp your greeting or other image on top of it. Adding a shadow stamp sets off your image and gives your card a finished look.

Make a shadow stamp to mimic the shape of your stamp. For example, if you have an image of a butterfly, cut the fun foam slightly larger, but in the same shape. Then use the foam as a shadow stamp and stamp your butterfly image on top. Want to play with shadow stamping? Jan's class Out of the Shadows on March 18 will teach you several shadowing techniques.

Have a great week!

Mary and Jan
To find out more about what's going on at The Super Scrapbook Store check our website: www.mydomainaname.com.

Want to contact us or unsubscribe? Email: youremailaddress@your domain.com.

We will never sell, share, or trade your personal information or email address. *Period.*

Figure 3.2   *(Continued)*

Hello, Gardening Friends!

Maintaining a nice lawn and landscape sure takes a lot of time out of our busy schedules. To help you, I've compiled a handy checklist of important spring gardening chores. Taking care of these things *now* will save you tons of time later on in the season when you want to be enjoying your yard, not slaving in it.

Spring Chore Checklist

- ❏ Put down weed preventer now.
- ❏ Apply bark mulch as soon as possible.
- ❏ Apply Scotts Halts or other crabgrass killer in the next two weeks.
- ❏ Fertilize all perennials, bulbs, and shrubs before the end of April.
- ❏ Edge beds with a spade as soon as possible to keep new grass from creeping in.
- ❏ Rake up dead grass areas and work in topsoil. Sow grass seed now.
- ❏ Toss out old soil in pots that you used last year.
- ❏ Put out slug bait.
- ❏ Spray ornamentals for fungus.
- ❏ Spray for galls on pine.

You can stop in the Great Garden Center to pick up any of the supplies you may need to complete these spring chores. And don't forget to grab some of our beautiful frost-friendly pansies to plant for extra color right now.

Easter Is Coming!

When you stop in, pick up an Easter egg from the basket. In your egg will be an Easter treat and a surprise slip for at least 20% and up to 50% off an item. How much will *you* save?!

Flowers make a thoughtful hostess gift or a joyful centerpiece for your Easter dinner. We are very excited to announce our new SIGNATURE BOUQUETS created by our talented floral designers. You can choose from *Carol's Classics* or *Maggie's Magic* for lovely spring arrangements.

Happy Gardening,

Jim Smith

Figure 3.3   **Sample Email.**

Rules of the Road for Email Marketing   A few rules of the road to follow when using email as a marketing tool make the information superhighway a little bit safer and more pleasant for everyone.

No Spam   Don't be a spammer. It gives everybody who uses email marketing appropriately a bad name. Spam is *any unsolicited email.*

The Can-Spam Act of 2003 makes it illegal to send spam. Keeping your email marketing in compliance with the Can-Spam Act is easy and should present absolutely no problem for anyone who is using this tool legitimately and with integrity. Here are the basics:

- The header information must be true and accurate. The "From" address must say who you really are, and don't hide your originating email address. Basically, don't lie.

- Don't use deceptive subject lines—they must reflect what's really in the email. So if you're sending your schedule of events, don't make the subject line "Message from Mom." Once again, no lying.

- Give the recipient the option to "unsubscribe" and stop receiving email from you. Immediately comply with any request to take someone off your list.

- Include information about who you are and give your contact information in the email.

That's it! If you want more complete information or to read the specific regulations, check on the government's website: http://www.ftc.gov/spam.

Opt-In Only   Make your list an "opt-in" only list. Opt-in means that you have asked to send, and your customer has agreed to receive, your email information.

Don't send your messages to anyone who hasn't opted-in to your list—even if they are a customer and your message is informational. This means your default is "send NO message" unless they have said yes to getting your email, rather than the default being "send email" unless they actively opt-out.

Unsubscribe Give your list members an opportunity to "unsubscribe" and stop getting email from you. This is easy to do automatically if you use an email "list server." It can also be done manually by simply including—at the bottom of *every* message—the line, "To stop getting emails from The Widget Wizard, Tom Jones, just reply to this message with Unsubscribe in the subject line."

Make sure you immediately take everyone who unsubscribes off the list.

Privacy Policy Have a clear privacy policy that explains what you will and won't do with your customer's email address. You might want to state your privacy policy at the bottom of each of your email messages and at the time you ask people to opt-in.

Here's what we suggest for your privacy policy. "We will never sell, barter, trade, or give your email address to anyone else, for any reason. Period. If you give it to us, it stays with us."

Customers will feel much better knowing their private email won't be sold or given to other people who probably *will* spam them.

Technical Tips for Email Marketing This section includes an overview of how to use technoogy to make your email marketing easier.

Build and Manage Your Email List There are basically two ways to send bulk email messages. One is to build a distribution list in the email program you are using now. Outlook, Outlook Express,

AOL, or Yahoo! are a few of the more popular ones. All have some kind of function for building a list with multiple names on it and then sending one message to everyone on the list.

This method is fine to start out with and to use until your list gets bigger—about 100 addresses or so. After that, the process of using the distribution list on your regular email program will quickly become unmanageable.

Your Internet Service Provider (ISP) may not let you send to very large groups. They will think you are spamming. Also when you start sending to large groups, the ISPs of the people receiving your messages may end up blocking them, also believing that they are spam.

Here's the solution. Get a "list host" (also called a "list server") with the software you need to build and manage your list and to send email messages. This will allow you to keep your address list on the Web (not on your hard drive in the office), access it from any computer in the world connected to the Internet, and send messages with the click of a button. These kinds of email marketing programs are superpowerful, fairly easy, and can really make email marketing work for you.

These list servers are usually cheap—under thirty bucks a month. You can't even buy the *postage* on 150 postcards for that amount of money, let alone the card itself, the printing, and the design. Only 150! I sure hope you have a bigger customer list than that. With a good email marketing program you can send virtually unlimited messages to any number of your customers.

Several good email programs are available, including the one we've developed especially for retailers, WhizBang! Email. This has all the features you need to create and manage your email database and create and send email marketing campaigns. It comes fully integrated with our WhizBang! Websites because, as you've read, we believe that email marketing is the best way to drive visitors to your website. WhizBang! Email also comes standalone for people who already have websites that they want to keep. Check it out at www.whizbangemail.com.

Sending Plain Text versus HTML Many email marketing programs will offer the choice to send your messages in HTML so that it shows up in the recipient's mailbox with beautiful graphics looking like a web page or in plain text. Here are the pros and cons of both types.

HTML Pros: There are some very clear benefits of sending emails in HTML. The messages just plain look better. You can add pictures, images, special formatting, color, all the same visual things you do in your store to brand your business. You can make your email look like your store! Sending pictures, whether they're of a product, a special event, or the employee of the month, is a really great way to make emotional connections with your customers.

HTML Cons: While the temptation to send email in goodlooking HTML might be great, it can cause problems. It takes a very long time to load those graphics if your customer is using a dial-up modem rather than some sort of broadband technology. If it takes too long, the message will likely be deleted before it's read. Also, HTML messages can look kind of slick and impersonal—more like an advertisement than a message from a friend.

The good news is that every month more and more people are upgrading their computers and moving to broadband technology. So more and more are able to read HTML emails quickly and easily.

Plain Text Pros: The biggest benefit of sending your email marketing messages in plain text is that it looks like an email sent from a friend. No one in your personal address book is sending you fancy HTML emails and one of the primary goals in your marketing is to create and enhance your personal relationships with your customers.

As a side note, *none* of the ubersuccessful direct marketers whom we hear from regularly are sending us emails in HTML. I doubt that it's because they haven't tried it or don't know how to do it (hah!), so I have to conclude that they continue to use plain text because it's effective. We've got no proof of this; it's a gut feeling.

Plain Text Cons: The cons of sending in plain text are, of course, the opposite of sending in HTML. You can't send pictures, you can't add color or images, and you can't use advanced formatting features that make your emails easy to read. To mitigate some of this problem and make your plain text message easier to read:

- Keep your paragraphs short.
- Use lines of ********, ^^^^^^^^^^, or ####### to separate thoughts or sections of your newsletter.
- Use ALL CAPS headlines for better scanability.
- Make sure there's enough white space for easy reading.
- Make each line no longer than 70 characters and use a hard break (the Enter key) between each line.

All of these details make your message easier to read and if it's easy to read, more of your customers will actually get it.

What's the bottom line on the HTML versus Plain Text debate? For most retailers the benefits of using HTML email outweigh the minuses. The trick is to keep your emails as personal, friendly, and simple as possible while still adding the visual elements that make HTML great.

Build a Template   If you send out a quarterly newsletter or a monthly tip, consider building a template. Create the basic structure of your message—the greeting, the body components, the signature, and the closing—the first time and then use it over and over again. All you have to do is type in the new content; the structure stays the same.

Create regular "columns." If you send a monthly newsletter, you might include a Quick Tip, a Schedule of Events, a featured product, an outside Resource of the Month, a funny (store-centered) Horoscope, and a personal letter from you. Do those same columns over and over each month and add something else only if you have a particular reason.

This template format has benefits for both you and your customer. For you, obviously, it's easier to compose the messages and get them out if you don't have to think about what to write each time. For your customers, it makes reading the messages easier if they can expect to find the same format each time.

Ask for a Referral/Send This to a Friend Forwarding an email message is really easy, and that makes it a great way for you to get referrals. Always ask your customers to forward your message to friends and family who might find them interesting or useful. Make the request part of your template. It's simple to do and could get you lots of new customers with no work or expense on your part.

Copywriting Tips for Email Success Quality writing is one of the most important factors to successful email marketing. Your message helps to differentiate you from your competitors and makes a lasting impression on your customers.

Writing for email is somewhat different from writing for print. The ease of hitting the Delete button and the competition for attention in the in-box makes it even more important to grab and hold your reader's attention, right from the start. Here are a few copywriting tips to help you make the most of your email marketing.

Subject Line The subject line is very important. It is essentially the *headline* for your email message. It is the first thing your customer sees when deciding whether to open and read your message.

If you want to grab the reader's attention, this is the place to do it. Here are a few tips for subject lines that get results:

- Be honest with your subject lines; don't bait and switch.
- Avoid phrases and words commonly used in spam, like *"free."*
- Be relevant.
- Show the value of your offer.
- Consider using personalization.
- Focus on the customer and their benefit, not on you or your company.

Go back and read the section on writing headlines in the special section called Copywriting for Retailers. The same techniques apply.

"From" Line   Like the subject line, the "from" name plays a crucial role in a recipient's decision to open your message—or hit the delete button. Many emails are deleted because recipients don't recognize the name of the sender. In the "from" line, put your company name, newsletter title, or your own name if it will be immediately recognizable.

Don't use your own name if most of your recipients won't recognize it and don't assume that they will. They may recognize your face, and even know your first name, but that might not translate into knowing your name in their in-box.

If your business name is Jim Smith Agency, using Jim Smith is a great idea for a "from" line. If your business name is Flowers Designed by Stephen, but your name is April—well, that doesn't work. In that case use the business name.

Don't repeat the "from" information in the subject line; that's just wasting valuable copy real estate. If you're sending a message from County Line Nursery, the subject shouldn't be County Line

Nursery News. They already know whom it's from. A better subject would include a benefit the customer will get by reading the newsletter: Pruning Guide and Perennial Planting Report Inside.

The email header would look like this:

To: Jane Jones

From: County Line Nursery News

Subject: Pruning Guide and Perennial Planting Report Inside

Short, but Sweet   Write concisely and state your purpose early in the email. Body copy should be brief, compelling, and immediately engaging. Because many readers skim their emails, it should be easy to determine the point of the message right from the start.

Scanability is important, so put key words or phrases in bold text. Only use underlining in your email or on your website if the text is a link.

Be Personal   Studies have shown that people generally prefer a more relaxed, conversational tone for email. Include words such as *you*, *we*, and *I*, rather than using your company name to make the message conversational. This first person writing style makes the message appear more comfortable and lets your customers connect with you on a one-to-one level.

The more you can get your readers to feel the personal connection to *you*, a person, not your business, the more powerful and effective all your messages will be. Make sure that all your emails are from a real person—you, your manager, a staff member—and signed with their name.

Make Your English Teacher Proud   Yes, your message does have to be free of spelling and grammatical errors. Spell check helps, but it doesn't do the hole job. See what I men? Neither one of these too (oops! three) errors are picked up with spell check. Proofread your copy carefully.

A good trick is to read your copy out loud after you've written it and check for a fluid, logical flow. Always have at least one other person check your copy to ensure it makes sense and is error free.

Business emails are not usually the place to use "netspeak," emoticons, or weird acronyms. LOL may mean "laughing out loud" to you, but your readers may think you've taken a dive off the deep end. Save your :-> and ;) for your FRNS, TYVM. (Translation: Save your devilish grins and winks for your friends, thank you very much!) The exception to this rule would be if your target market is trendy teens or techno-geeks.

Get Personal   Consider using personalization within your email. By using a first name or inserting individualized custom content, your customer will feel like you understand their needs. Personalization is a great way to increase customer loyalty and the success of your email marketing.

One potential down side to this technique is that customers don't always enter the correct information into the fields when they are signing up online. This could lead to a strange greeting like "Dear staniswitcz," instead of the "Dear Jim," you were hoping for. A greeting like this makes the message feel more robotic and *less* personal rather than friendly and *more* personal.

Give Them What They Want   Great copywriting aside, if you don't have a valuable offer or compelling content, your customers are not going to read your emails. Don't send emails just for the sake of emailing. Make sure that each message you send has valuable, relevant information and offers.

Call To Action   Always include a specific call to action to ensure that the reader knows the next step. If you want recipients to visit your website, insert a link; if you want them to call and schedule an appointment, include the phone number. Make the call to action prominent so that it gets noticed, even if the reader is skimming.

Your Email Signature File This is a little sidebar to the email marketing conversation that can help turn *all* of your emails into minimarketing messages.

Always have a signature file at the end of every email you send—not just the ones to your customer list—with your name, business name, address, phone, fax, website address, and an *invitation to sign up for your newsletter* or to *visit your website*. Here's what our signature file looks like.

Susan Negen | WhizBang! Training
212 South Harbor #301 Grand Haven, MI 49417
616 842 4237 | www.whizbangtraining.com

SIGN UP ↑

You are invited to subscribe to our FREE email Tip of the Week - It's filled with practical business building information!

Nice, huh? Of course, yours doesn't have to be fancy; it just has to have the necessary information. Here's the text version of our signature file:

Bob Negen

WhizBang! Training

212 S. Harbor Dr. #301

Grand Haven, MI 49417

Phone: 616-842-4237

Fax: 616-842-2977

www.whizbangtraining.com

Get your *free* WhizBang! Tip of the Week via email.

Click here to sign up.

One of the great things about a signature file is that you can create it once and then set up your email program to automatically include it at the end of every email. You don't have to think about it—your minimarketing message simply shows up.

Not only is this a wonderful marketing idea, it's just plain professional. Adding your contact information as a signature file on every email is a baseline professional standard. If you don't know how to set up a signature file for your email system, check the Help program. It's easy to do.

Just Do It   There's no question about it. Email marketing is one of the most powerful, effective, easy, fun, and inexpensive tactics in this whole book. Just do it.

A Personal Invitation   We have used email marketing for many, many years to build close, lasting relationships with our clients, and we would like to have you as one of our business friends, too. *Your* personal invitation to sign up for the WhizBang! Tip of the Week is on the opposite page.

Shop More Often Tactic #7: Make Your Website a Resource for Your Customers

Your website is the perfect tool to become a broader resource to your customers. Use your website to be the trusted expert, be a clearinghouse for information, and keep your customers involved emotionally with the community by sharing human interest news.

Set Up a Special Section or Even Several Sections on Your Site
It's important to make your resources section easy to find. Don't make your customers work to find all the great information you've made available to them. Promote it on your homepage, give the sec-

---

This is your personal invitation to get the FREE "WhizBang! Tip of the Week," an email message to inform, encourage, and inspire.

We promise our tips will be short, practical, profitable, and fun. Our tips are kind of like a good cup of coffee—a mid-week professional pick-me-up. Here's a sample of the nuts and bolts information you'll receive:

Tip of the Week # 141

TIP*********TIP*********TIP********TIP*********TIP*********TIP*********TIP

The individuals who apply for employment at your company are not only job candidates, but are frequently also your customers (or their friends, parents, and relatives are).

For this reason, and a host of others, it is important to remember that candidates who are not hired (whether they were interviewed or not) deserve courtesy and respect.

SEND A "SORRY" LETTER

Or mail a postcard, or make a quick phone call to everyone who took the time to fill out an application but wasn't hired. It's polite, it's good customer service, and it's good marketing.

If you want a sample and template "sorry" letter to use in your business, just email us at tips@whizbangtraining.com. We'll send it right out to you.

TIP*********TIP*********TIP********TIP*********TIP*********TIP*********TIP

To sign up, go to our website www.whizbangtraining.com and enter your name and email address in the sign-up box. We look forward to having you as part of the gang!

---

tion its own tab on your primary navigation options, and place links back to this section throughout the site. Don't be shy, promote it.

Getting Great Content The information on your website, also called its content, does not have to be original. You or your staff don't have to create it. It just has to be interesting or helpful to your customers.

You can get customers to write articles, reviews, and columns. You can hire a college student to interview well-known personalities in your field. You can create a "staff's picks" section—the list goes on and on.

Of course, if you are trying to become the trusted expert, it helps if you write most of the articles, tips, and reviews yourself—but is not a requirement. It's more important to have a content-rich website that gets visited often than a completely original website where every word has come straight from your pen.

Articles   You know what makes your customers tick, you talk to them every day. These topics that they want to chat about are the subjects for great articles. If you own a pet store and you get lots of questions about the basics of dog training, you have the subject for an article. If you own a sewing store and your customers want to know what features on a sewing machine fit their style of sewing, you have a subject. If you have a bike shop and your customers want to know how to repair their bikes during a long ride, you have the subject for an article. Listen to your customers closely and you'll never run out of ideas for articles.

Hot Tip!

One way to get great content is to hire a freelance writer. There are many online services that match writers with people who have writing projects. Go to the Retailer Resources page on our website free resources page for information about some of these services that could work for you.

If you are not a good writer or if you can't find the time, hire someone to write your content. You may be able to find a customer who is a good writer and would be willing to trade their time for your products. In addition to being able to work for trade, the upside of hiring a customer is that that person will already know your products and probably has a passion that will shine through the articles they write.

The downside is if things don't work out as planned, you will have hurt feelings and you may even lose a customer.

If you choose to try to find a customer to help you with your writing, you can advertise the position with in-store posters and bag stuffers and post it on your website.

Calendars Having calendars filled with events of interest to your customers is a great way to be a broader resource, bring your customers back to your website more often, and attract hot prospects.

Post more than your own store events; post any events that your customers might find interesting, helpful, or fun. If you own a garden center, post all the classes that a gardener might find of interest, including master gardening classes, seminars hosted by your local agricultural cooperative, and even events at other garden centers. If you own an art gallery or your customer base is filled with people who appreciate the arts, post all the fine arts events in your area. If you have a toy store, you could list all the family-friendly activities in your town.

Think beyond your local events when you're creating your calendar. Your customers would probably dream about attending that big international conference where all the cool stuff is shown and all the cool people are seen and would love to know more about how to attend.

Feed their interests and fuel their desires to become more involved.

Archives An archive is defined as "a place where historical documents are preserved." Having an archive for your newsletter, either paper or email, is a wonderful way to make your website more interesting and add content with very little extra work.

You've already created the content; it makes sense to keep using it. Organize your archives by subject, chronologically, or any other way that makes sense to your customers. At our website www.whizbangtraining.com we organize our information by skill sets so if you come to our site you can easily search our article archives by topic—marketing, staff development, inventory management, or store operations.

If you own a bookstore, sort your staff picks by genre, by author, or by staff reviewer. If you own a gift shop selling home accessories, sort your home decorating tips by season, by parts of the home, or chronologically. If you have a store that sells outdoor gear, sort your articles by season, by activity, or chronologically.

Making your site easier to use and more interesting will keep your customers coming back more often, will prompt them to send their friends to your site, and will result in more sales on your site and in your store.

Teach Tips and Techniques   Develop your customers' skills and you'll sell your customers more stuff. It's really that simple. The better your customers are at doing whatever you sell, the more they will buy and the more often they will buy it.

At the Mackinaw Kite Co. we were experts at "skill development." We taught people how to be better kite fliers through free kite flying lessons every Tuesday night at the beach. We had a Pro-Spinners Club that brought kids together to practice, play, and learn new tricks on their yo-yos. We had game tables set out in the store to teach people how to play the games we sold.

Take this idea of skill development and use it to make your website an interesting and useful resource for your customers. If you own a garden center, have a Great Garden Tips section. If you have a sewing shop, have a section on sewing tips.

Hot Tip!

Putting streaming audio and video on your website is getting easier every day. This is the technology wave of the future and you'd better get ready to ride it!

Go to our Retailer Resources page on our website www.whizbangtraining.com to learn about recommended audio and visual products and services for your website.

Use photos whenever you can and *even use audio or video to make the lesson more meaningful.* There's no doubt that actually watching a video of you doing an advanced technique is more powerful and more interesting than reading about it.

Provide Links to Other Sites with Worthwhile Information Sending your customers to other websites with information of interest to them is a great way to be a broader resource. Giving your customers the opportunity to check out other high-quality sources of great information shows them that you are open and generous. It may take them away from your website but it will bring them back to it more often in the future.

Here are a couple of tips to make this strategy work harder for you:

First, as we mentioned in the section on building a great website, always have the link open a new browser session. That means that your site will stay open in one window and the other site will open up in a new window. If you don't do this, when your customer clicks on the link, the new website opens in the place of your site. Essentially your site disappears.

It's not difficult to do; just ask the person who maintains your website to make sure this happens. Tell them you need "new browser sessions." If they don't know what you're talking about, find a new person.

Second, when you link to a site, contact them to inquire if there is any information they would like you to include and see if they are interested in putting your link on their site. Having "reciprocal links" will increase your website traffic by giving you access to another site's visitors.

Shop More Often Tactic #8: Use Email Campaigns to Sell Related Products

Selling your customers everything they need to enjoy their hobby, have a successful experience with your products, or get the most from their purchase is a great way to give great service and build your average sale at the same time.

In your store you have a salesperson talking to your customers, asking questions, and helping your customer buy the right product. Unfortunately, when selling on your website you don't have the personal give and take with your customers you have with them in your store. That doesn't mean they won't benefit from all the wonderful add-ons you suggest when you have face-to-face interaction. They probably want the stuff, and I assume you want the sale.

One solution is to send your customer an email—or series of emails—about products related to the ones they just bought on your website. This kind of email gives you the opportunity to sell them everything they should have bought in the first place. It's a great way to prompt them to shop with you again.

Of course if you are incredibly organized and disciplined, you can send these emails manually one at a time, but frankly we haven't met a retailer yet who is this organized and patient. An easier, hands-off way to get the job done is to set up an *automatic* email campaign.

An automatic email campaign is a series of emails set to be sent out at predetermined times based on the particular item that a customer buys. In many website shopping carts email campaign capabilities are integrated into the programming, including WhizBang! Websites.

Let's say you are an outdoor outfitter. You sell hiking boots, backpacks, camping accessories, tents, and other outdoor gear. After someone buys a backpack from your website you could preprogram a campaign that might go something like this:

1. *Email #1*—One week after the sale: "You should have received your backpack by now. If you haven't, call us right away and we'll help you track it."

2. *Email #2*—Two weeks after the sale: "We hope you're enjoying your new backpack. Please don't hesitate to call if you have any questions or if we can be of any help at all. By the way, our staff, who are all avid backpackers, highly recommend this sleeping bag."

3. *Email #3*—Five weeks after the sale: "We hope you've been spending lots of time on the trail with your new backpack. If you don't care for most of the freeze dried food out there, come on in and we'll send you home with a free pouch of our new Chef's Choice Freeze Dried Wonder trail food. We guarantee after you try it you'll never carry anything else again."

Each of these messages should also contain a link that sends them back to something interesting on your website. You might send them to a Staff's Favorite Trails section or maybe a section containing reports on trail conditions.

Think past the first online purchase and find ways to proactively build your relationship with that customer, add value to their purchase, and sell them more great stuff.

Keep Your Customers for Life

Six Key Concepts to Keep Customers for Life

These key concepts focus on the slow but steady building of your customer base to massive proportions. It's about never losing customers once you've got them.

Key Concept #1: Keep Your Customers for as Many Years as Possible

For several years the Mackinaw Kite Co. rented a storefront from Paul Fortino, an outstanding gentleman and second generation merchant who owned the European style gourmet food store next to ours. Paul sold candy of all types, good imported pastas, meats, cheeses, beer, wine, and liquor.

Paul taught us many lessons in the years we knew him. One day he shared one of his secrets to success with Bob. "I sell candy to children who come in with their parents. When they become teenagers, I sell them their pop. When they turn 21 years old, I sell them their first six pack of beer. When they become older adults, I sell them fine food and good wine. Then eventually I start selling their children candy."

Paul understood the concept of "womb to tomb." He kept customers for their entire lives. Not every store has a product mix that can retain a customer through the course of an entire lifetime, but it pays to keep your customers for as many years as possible. Boy, does it pay. This is one of the most profitable ways for any retailer to build their business.

When you keep your customers for more years, your customer base grows more efficiently because you don't have to constantly replace customers you've lost. New customers become net gains in the size of your customer base, rather than mere replacements for customers you've lost. Get a customer—keep a customer!

Key Concept #2: Never Take Your Customers for Granted

There is a tendency in all long-term relationships to begin to feel too comfortable and take each other for granted. Don't let it happen with your customers.

Bob recently spoke to a musician who told him about the store where he bought his first drum set. He went on to become a professional musician and of course bought more drums, sticks, and all the other accoutrements of a professional drummer. One day he went into the store and although the owners greeted him by name, they never left the work they were doing to help him. He left, went to the music store down the street, and never went back.

His statement was, "They acted like they didn't care. They knew I was going to buy something, so they didn't bother helping me." Not only did they lose a good customer, but their competition down the road gained a great new customer.

You can never, ever get too comfortable in any relationship with a customer. If anything, the opposite is true; the longer they stay with you, the harder you should work to keep the relationship fresh, interesting, and exciting.

Key Concept #3: Be Constant

Stick with your customers. Be like that person who is always there when you need a friend. Be a constant part of their lives. Constantly show them you care. Constantly give them a reason to shop with you. Constantly prove to them you deserve their business.

Every quality touch is like a deposit in a bank account. Just like building a real bank account filling with real money, if you keep making deposits, sooner or later you'll be rich. Only instead of having a bank account full of money you'll have an account filled with customer loyalty.

This is what you need in today's hypercompetitive retail market—full accounts with your customers. When you've earned the kind of loyalty that comes from dozens, if not hundreds, of quality touches you don't have to be afraid when Wal-Mart moves in down the road, when your top supplier becomes your competition by selling online, or when a national franchise moves into your territory.

Developing this type of loyalty in your customers is a constant effort, but an effort that pays enormous dividends.

Key Concept #4: Be Consistent

People don't like to be surprised. They crave consistency. Think about McDonald's. Hardly any people think that McDonald's makes the best hamburger in the world, and yet they've sold billions and billions of them. Why? Because their product is consistent. A Big Mac tastes the same in Anchorage and Arkansas, in New York and New Brunswick. Although there are local variations on the theme, the McDonald's experience is pretty consistent throughout the world.

People would rather have a pretty good experience all of the time than have an incredible experience one visit and a lousy experience the next. When you train your staff to give consistently great service, keep a consistent merchandising philosophy, and keep your marketing messages consistent your customers will stay with you because they feel comfortable doing business with you. The value of this comfort cannot be overestimated.

Key Concept #5: Keep Your Approach to Your Business Fresh and Exciting

It seems counterintuitive to follow two sections suggesting you keep your customers' experiences constant and consistent with a section that suggests you keep your approach fresh and exciting.

It's not. Just as the best garden needs pruning, the best wardrobe needs sprucing up, and the greatest music collection needs updating, your business needs to constantly grow and improve.

The first several years the Mackinaw Kite Co. was open, it was strictly a kite shop. We were kite purists and proud of it. One day Bob's good friend Bert suggested that he start selling toys. Bob was aghast, shocked, to think someone would suggest he sell toys. He owned a *kite* store after all.

At some point, paying the rent became more important than the purity of the kite selection and the Mackinaw Kite Co. started to sell toys. It quickly became one of the most recognized toy stores in Michigan. Change can be good.

Very Important Point: Your customers vote with their wallets. The amount of money in your register tells you loudly and clearly whether they approve of the changes you're making in your business.

On a different note it's important for you as a businessowner to remain fresh and excited about being an entrepreneur. One motivation to keep things fresh is to keep your customers interested in staying with you. Another motivation is to keep your own professional life interesting and exciting. A bored owner runs a boring store, stocked with boring merchandise, staffed by bored employees.

It's important that you go to trade shows, educational seminars, buy tapes, read books, join mastermind groups, and stay intellectually and emotionally involved in your business. Retail is a contact sport and if you want to be successful, it's important to stay in the game.

Stay up-to-date with all the latest technology and understand how you can use it to build your business. Nothing stays the same and in today's world change is coming more rapidly than ever. Stay on top of it if you hope to thrive.

Key Concept #6: What's a Customer Worth? Show Me the Money!

What are your customers worth? There are lots of ways to look at that question, but here's one very simple equation to measure the value of your customer base:

$$\text{Average \$ sale} \times \text{average transactions per month}$$
$$\times \text{average number of months}$$
$$\times \text{number of customers}$$
$$= \textit{value of your customer base}$$

The real power in your marketing efforts is to work on *all four of those different ways to grow your business at once.* If you work only on one part of the equation, you have to make an enormous change to make a difference. But if you make small, incremental improvements in all four areas, however, "*Bam!!*" as Emeril would say. You'll see the power of incremental growth.

Exploring the Power of Incremental Growth   Here's an example for the fictional company, Gertrude's Gifts. Currently Gertrude has 500 active customers with an average sale of $25, her customers shop on average once every 8 months, and they continue to buy from her for 24 months before they stop buying from her.

	Current	Potential
Average dollars per sale	$25/transaction	$27.5/transaction
Average transactions per month	1 transaction/ 8 months	1 transaction/ 6 months
Average lifespan of the customer	24 months	30 months
Number of customers	500 customers	550 customers
Value of Gertrude's customer base	$37,500	$60,500
Increase in customer base value		62%

In the "potential" scenario Gertrude makes four *small* incremental improvements:

1. Increases her average sale by just 10 percent—only $2.50 on average. That's one extra $10 add-on to every fourth customer. Not such a big stretch.

2. Gets her customers to buy from her once every *six* months instead of once every eight months.

3. Keeps her customers shopping with her just six months longer before they go away.

4. Increases her number of customers by 10 percent—just 50 new customers, less than one a week.

Bam!! A 62 percent increase in the value of her customer base.

If Gertrude had worked on only one of the elements—say, improving her average sale—she would have had to raise it $15.50, from $25 to $40.50, to see the same sales growth. That's *a lot* harder than raising it $2.50 to $27.50.

What does this mean for *you* financially? If you really want some intense motivation, take the time to fill out the following table for your business. Add in some small, incremental improvements and see what your number is.

	Current	**Potential**
Average dollars per sale		
Average transactions per month		
Average lifespan of the customer		
Number of customers		
Value of Gertrude's customer base		
Increase in customer base value		

Now think for just a minute about what that number would mean for your business and for you personally. Motivated yet?

Working on these four components together is really powerful, and they are all a function of building close, personal, and lasting relationships with your customers. Luckily, that's our primary advantage over the big box and Internet competition.

Three Terrific Tactics to Keep Customers for Life

If you're constantly losing customers after one or two transactions it won't matter how many new customers you bring in the front end. To build a successful, profitable business you have to keep your customers buying from you year, after year, after year. These two tactics will help you stay focused on the real money-making marketing activities—keeping your customers more active for more years.

Terrific Tactic #1: Build a Marketing Plan

Have you ever found yourself thinking, That promotion really worked great, how come we quit doing it? We have, and so have most of the retailers we know.

It's what we affectionately refer to as RADD—Retailers' Attention Deficit Disorder. We run from one idea to another chasing a buck and in the process end up abandoning lots of things that have worked in the past or would have worked if we had given them the proper time and attention.

It can't be stated strongly enough: To keep your customers coming back year after year, keep using the marketing tactics that work.

One of the ways to make sure all the things you did in the

past keep getting done and still add in your new ideas is to make a marketing plan. Remember this old adage, "If it ain't written, it ain't real."

Committing your ideas, concepts, and plans to paper imposes discipline on your thinking, which is invaluable, not to mention the fact that it helps you remember what you've done and when and how you did it.

Create a separate document for each of the tactics you plan to use. Some of your tactics will by their nature be very simple and have very little that needs to be planned; others will be complicated and take lots of planning and work.

Don't let perfection get in the way of progress!

The important thing is to get some of your ideas down on paper now. Start with a quick description of your idea, a rough outline of an implementation plan, or a sketch of your promotional piece. As you start to work with your plan, to find out what works, and to go through the steps of implementing each tool, you'll get smarter and can add information about that tool to your plan.

Here are some things you may want to consider:

- What's my goal for this tactic: Get new customers? Engender loyalty? A specific sales goal? Get a repeat visit from existing customers?
- What are the steps I need to take in the beginning, middle, and end of this process?
- How much will this cost me?
- How will I let my customers know about this?
- How will I train my employees about this tactic?
- How will I evaluate the success of this tactic?

A Word about Budgets   Now let me admit that our philosophy about marketing budgets is contrary to what most other people teach. That's because we're driven by opportunities, by challenges—by reality.

Big companies are like freighters; they have enormous power because of their size. It's their competitive advantage. We small businesses are like those little inflatable Zodiacs. Our competitive advantage is being able to change direction on a dime, to change speeds almost instantly, and to go places where the big boys can't.

> When we, as entrepreneurs, see an opportunity we need to act on it. Now.
>
> If we do something and it works like a charm, we need to roll it out. Now.
>
> If we try something and it sinks like a big round rock, we need to stop doing it. Now.

A hard-and-fast budget is a good tool for big companies. What *you* need is a clear understanding of what you can afford to invest and a burning desire to make sure every penny you spend counts.

Here's how I suggest you look at your marketing budget. Take 3 to 5% of your sales and create an "investment fund." For the sake of illustration, let's say your annual sales are $100,000. You decide to invest 3% of your annual sales into marketing. So you're willing to invest $3,000 in your marketing efforts.

But since you look at marketing as an investment, not a cost, you get to reinvest "profits" when something works. So if you spend $500 on an endorsed mailing and it generates a profit of $1,500 you don't deduct the $500 you've spent from your investment fund. In fact, you might want to add some of those profits back into your marketing fund and *you definitely want to immediately look for other similar partners for more endorsed mailing opportunities.*

When something works, reinvest, and continue to reinvest until you start to see diminishing returns. If a promotion was success-

ful, do it again. If your customers enjoyed your Customer Appreciation Day, do it every year. If your rewards program is well received,
make sure everyone on your staff gets behind it. If you have a successful promotional partnership with one school, try to partner
with every other school in town. If you got a good response to the
Jigsaw Puzzle Promotion, do it again next year or maybe even try it
twice next year. If your seminars keep filling up, schedule more.

Win Some, Lose Some   Now let's talk about tools you've chosen
that have a disappointing return. I know I stated that if something doesn't work, you should abandon it. And you should. But
before you abandon any marketing tool that you feel really good
about, take a good, solid look at it and try to understand why it
didn't work.

Could the headline be improved? Was the price wrong? Was
the offer wrong? Was the endorsed mailing sent to the wrong
group of people? Was the denomination on the gift certificate too
low? Was the promotion held at the wrong time of year? Was the
graphic design so ugly that people didn't take the promotional
piece seriously?

The important thing to realize is that if you felt good about it
make sure you give that tool a real solid look and perhaps give it a
second chance. Trust your instincts—they are usually pretty solid.
Treat every good marketing idea as a seed. It may look small but
with the proper care and attention, it will grow and provide you
with something wonderful.

Even if you choose not to set and stick by a budget, think
through the costs involved with every tool you choose to use. Understanding the financial implications, both the costs and possible
returns, is part of the process of fleshing out each tactic.

Yearly Review   Setting some time aside each year to review your
marketing plan, to check out your mix of tactics, to recap what

worked and what didn't is the best way we know of to maintain a continuous flow of amazing marketing aimed at building great customer relationships.

Figure 4.1 can help you review your mix of tactics.

If you don't take time to make and manage a marketing plan, you will probably fall victim to RADD and miss repeating some of your best tactics. Your customers will miss them. Do all you can to keep customers for more years by continuing your best tactics. If they're working—don't stop!

Terrific Tactic #2: Track the Effectiveness of Your Marketing Efforts

There's an old saying, "If you can measure it, you can manage it and if you can manage it you can improve it." As your Marketer's Mindset matures you'll naturally become more interested in the results of what you do. And your interest will become more specific.

"That worked pretty well" will be replaced with "Our average sale increased 22% during the promotion." You'll start to track the real costs involved with your efforts including the labor involved. You'll track the number of new customers your efforts attract in addition to the sales they generated. You'll see past the immediate results and see how all of your efforts create long-term value for your company.

There are several things you can track with your marketing efforts. A partial list includes:

- Cost (including labor).
- Average sale.
- Largest sale.

Tactics	Increase average sale	Increase number of transactions per year	Increase number of years	Get new customers	Adds customers to my database	Continuous tactic	Weekly tactic	Monthly tactic	One-time event	Put your own strategy or goal here
Preferred Customer Club	X	X	X		X	X				

Figure 4.1 Reviewing Your Mix of Tactics.

- Number of transactions.
- Number of new customers as measured by new names acquired.
- Sales increase over last week.
- Sales increase over last year.
- Return on investment.
- Publicity generated.
- Goodwill generated (strictly subjective, but important nonetheless).

As you become more sophisticated in your tracking efforts and you make improvements based on your findings, you will naturally see things work smoother, produce better returns, and become more effective. This all adds up to a better customer experience that increases the number of years they keep shopping with you.

Terrific Tactic #3: Fight "Perceived Indifference" Tooth and Nail

Although this is really an attitude and not technically a tactic, it needs to be mentioned because it is the single most important thing you can do to keep your customers coming back to your store year after year: *Showing your customers how much you value them should be your number one priority.*

The tactics you choose depend on your industry, your customer base, and your resources. But you *must* keep your customers front and center in your business consciousness and make every encounter with them an opportunity to show them how much you care.

CONCLUSION

Are You Interested or Are You Committed?

Congratulations on finishing the book! We sincerely hope your mind has been stretched and you are excited about becoming a New Millennium Merchant. Developing your Marketer's Mindset, loving your customers, and having fun in your store is a great way to make a living!

But ideas and excitement don't put cash in the bank. You must turn your new possibilities into your new reality. Gathering information is a start, but putting your new ideas into action is where the rubber meets the road. This book contains powerful information that hundreds of retailers like you have used to increase sales, create a buzz, and make retailing more fun—but you have to use it.

Being interested in success is not enough. It takes commitment. A commitment to spending the time. A commitment to spending the money. A commitment to continually grow.

What Next?

The first thing to do is build your customer list. The minute you get back on the floor of your store, start collecting the names, addresses, and email addresses of your customers. Do everything you can to get as many names as possible. Of course you want to respect the wishes of the people who don't want to share their contact information with you, but do all you can to build your list as quickly as you can.

Pick one or two tactics that really got you excited and start using them or start the planning. Get started. Momentum is important. Remember, don't let perfection get in the way of progress.

Write a plan. It doesn't have to be fancy. It just has to get done. Plain paper is fine, but if it ain't written, it ain't real. Those pieces of paper or that computer file will be the foundation of all your marketing efforts in the future. Each year you'll use your plan as a way to evaluate the successes and challenges of the past and use them to build a better plan for the future.

Enroll in Bob's Marketing Mentor Program. Bob will work with you to build a killer marketing plan that fits your market, your budget, your store, and your personality. Hundreds of your colleagues are Marketing Mentor alumni and report that sales are up and business is *fun*! You get a better-than-money-back guarantee so you have nothing to lose and *lots* to gain. To learn more, go to www.MarketingMentorProgram.com.

Finally, never stop learning. Re-read this book. Read another book. Foster your curiosity. Subscribe to business magazines. Treat your car like a rolling university and listen to audio recordings while you drive. Attend lots of seminars, which let you step away from the daily grind and really allow you to immerse yourself in a subject.

Get excited about learning! The world is constantly changing and the only way to keep up is to keep changing, too.

We want to thank you for giving us your time. Our sincerest hope is that you take this information and use it to make a difference in your life, your business, and your community.

Most of all, we want you to attain great success and have *fun*!

Best regards,

INDEX

HICKMANS